Change and Tradition
Cultural and Historical Perspectives

# Nigeria: Change and Tradition in an African State

Third Edition

William Neher
BUTLER UNIVERSITY

*Copley Publishing Group*
Acton, Massachusetts 01720

Printed in the United States of America

ISBN 1-58390-004-7

# CONTENTS

# INTRODUCTION

Africans, like other peoples of the world, inhabit a present which emerged from a unique past and is moving toward an uncertain future. For Africans, as for all other peoples, this cultural dynamic has existed from the beginning. Tradition in Africa, like tradition everywhere, has always renewed itself in response to change. Yet when Western scholars have spoken of African societies as traditional, they have all too often implied thereby that such societies are static, either not subject to change or unresponsive to its imperatives. When Europeans first began to acquaint themselves with African peoples, they assumed that they had "discovered" people who had been frozen in time. The Nigerian novelist Chinua Achebe despairs of this Western view of his land and people. In his critique of Joseph Conrad's *Heart of Darkness,* Achebe asserts that Conrad perpetuates a view of Africans as unchanging and unchanged ("An Image of Africa: Racism in Conrad's Heart of Darkness" in Achebe's *Hope and Impediments: Selected Essays,* New York, Doubleday, 1989). Such a perspective fails to take account of the dynamic nature of African tradition. In Africa, tradition has never been static. Instead, it has responded to changing conditions of many kinds, in a continuing struggle to sustain both the glory of the past and the vitality of the present.

Africa is a huge continent of over 500 million inhabitants, divided today into over fifty different political units. The people can further be divided into as many as 3,000 cultural and linguistic groups. Despite such diversity, definitions of Africans by non-Africans frequently invoke the physical characteristics of race as the single unifying factor of a continent of peoples. According to Ali Mazrui, Kenyan scholar and narrator of the acclaimed public television series, *The Africans,* racial homogeneity among Africans has been overemphasized by Western observers, while commonalties of situation and experience have been ignored. To understand these shared circumstances, physical and cultural, indigenous and externally imposed, is to begin a journey toward a more complete and more accurate view of what being African means and has meant to Africans.

Shared circumstances are given by ecology and by history. The lands of Africa tend to be harsh and difficult—receiving either too much rain (in the rain forests), or too little (in the deserts and savannas). Soils are often infertile; insects and parasites prey upon crops and herds, making food production difficult. All but two enclaves on the continent were suddenly annexed by European powers at the end of the nineteenth century and the beginning of the twentieth, meaning that nearly all Africans have had to deal, as a part of their recent past, with the political and social problems of being colonized. Most African nations have achieved independence only recently, and then not on the basis of traditional ethnic distinctions but on the basis instead of political boundaries fixed by the colonizing countries.

Nigeria, the focus of our study of African tradition and change, is one of the new nations of Africa—the most populous and potentially one of the most powerful. Like the rest of Africa, it is ethnically and culturally diverse (some estimates place the number of languages spoken in Nigeria at about 250). Within its borders is represented what Mazrui refers to as the "Triple Heritage" of Africa: the African, the Islamic, and the Christian. Each of these three traditions comprises not only a distinct religious ethos but also an entire cultural milieu—linguistic, political, and material. Islam and Christianity represent the outside forces that have shaped modern African cultures, in combination with traditional religions and indigenous world views. The northern half of Nigeria is largely Islamic, while in the southern half Christian and traditional beliefs dominate. Estimates suggest that about 49% of Nigeria's population is Muslim; about 34.5% are Christian; and about 18% follow traditional African religions.

Even the geographical configuration we now know as Nigeria reflects this triple heritage. There was no "nation" of Nigeria before 1912, when the country was created by the combination of two British colonized territories without regard to existing ethnic, political, or cultural identifications. The very name of the country was supplied by an outsider, Englishwoman Flora Shaw, who later married Frederick Lugard, the most famous colonial administrator of Nigeria. In these and other ways, Nigeria encapsulates the tensions and the problems characteristic of the continent as a whole.

This text focuses on three important ethnic groups of Nigeria—the Hausa of the North, the Yoruba of the Southwest, and the Igbo of the Southeast. Our study of these groups, the three largest in the country, will underscore the diversity, richness, and complexity of Africa and, at the same time, examine how these cultures have dealt with the changes wrought by colonialism and early modern nationalism.

As we begin, some terms and usages should be clarified. First, the term *tribe* or *tribal* does not appear often in this text because the term is of uncertain meaning and often carries negative connotations. Where classification is necessary, ethnic or linguistic markers are preferred, though even these are modern contrivances which do not always correspond well to patterns of self-identification in traditional Africa. The word *Yoruba,* for example, is of Hausa origin, and was used by the Hausa to refer to the great empire of Oyo. The people who founded Oyo, and whom we now call Yoruba, often referred to themselves as *Oluku mi,* meaning *my friend.* The Hausa themselves have been referred to by many different names in history; the Fulani, who became closely associated with the Hausa in Nigeria, call them the *Habe.* The word *Hausa,* from the Kanuri language of northeastern Nigeria, means west, indicating that the Hausa lived west of the Kanuri. The word *Igbo,* from the Kwa languages of West Africa, has been variously translated as *forest-dweller* or *community* and may once have referred to a much larger group of people speaking related languages.

What, then, does ethnic identification mean? Usually, ethnicity refers to a complex of cultural practices, including language, kinship organization, economic activities, location, types of dwellings, and religious practices. Once we have become better acquainted with the geography and great kingdom history of West Africa, we shall return to our study of ethnicity by taking a closer look at community life among the Hausa, the Yoruba, and the Igbo.

# GEOGRAPHICAL SETTING

Africa is the second largest continent, after Asia. It is three times larger than Europe and four times larger than the area of the United States. The coast of Africa has comparatively few gulfs or bays, however, with the result that the coastline itself appears shorter in total length than that of any other continent. Theories of tectonic plate movement suggest that the present African continent was at one time the center of a giant continent, from which the other continents have gradually drifted away. The African plate became isolated from the others, so that it has not been shaped by collisions with or passage of other plates, except in the northeastern corner where the Eurasian plate has had some effect, creating mountain ranges in the Ethiopia region.

## Physical Features

The interior of the continent is marked by several shallow basins that can be picked out on a contour map (see Map A, at end of text). These basins are marked by drainage systems that have become associated with great river systems. Geographers over the years have remarked that a peculiarity of these rivers is that they all seem to take very indirect routes to their oceans. The Niger River of West Africa, from which Nigeria takes its name, flows first toward the Sahara Desert before taking a sudden turn to the south and thence out to the Atlantic through modern day Nigeria. Similarly, the Congo River flows north until it takes a sweeping turn to flow back south and west toward the Atlantic. The Zambezi River of Southern Africa appears headed for the Kalahari Desert before taking an abrupt turn toward the Indian Ocean. Lake Chad, on the northern border of Nigeria, represents the drainage of a basin that never developed an outlet to an ocean (similar to the formation of Great Salt Lake in Utah).

As a result of these basins surrounded by ridges (escarpments), most of the rivers are broken by waterfalls and the rapids of cataracts where the rivers have cut their way through the ridges near the edges of the continent. Upriver travel into the African interior has been difficult historically because of these cataracts and falls. Still within the interior of the continent, rivers have often provided for ready movement of peoples. The Niger River, for example, in the region studied in this text, was a highway for trade and communication for several large African empires. A look at a physical map reveals that the southern third of the continent is nearly surrounded by the "Great Escarpment," where the edge of the ridges reaches almost to the sea. Features such as this and the escarpments of the Great Rift Valley in East Africa have constituted barriers to human movement and communication over the years.

[See Map A]

Climatic variations have also played a role in determining human movement and habitation on the African continent. From north to south, successive zones are increasingly arid and desert-like, next increasingly wet and tropical (in the Congo River Basin), and once again increasingly dry to desert-like, as in the Namib and Kalahari Deserts of Southern Africa. Between the arid and tropical zones lies the savanna that is characteristic of much of sub-Saharan Africa. A savanna is open country with scattered trees and vegetation, similar to the dryer parts of the Great Plains in the United States. Note that the dry grass savanna and the woodland savanna areas dominate most of Map B. The wettest or most tropical areas are found both at the coasts of East and West Africa and in the area of eastern Congo, the huge area drained by the Congo or Zaire River System.

The northern third of the continent is dominated by the Sahara Desert, part of an immense desert that stretches across the continents from Morocco to southern Pakistan and on to the Gobi Desert of Mongolia. The Namib Desert of Southern Africa reflects the mirror image of the global climatic feature that brought about the Sahara of the North. The Sahara provides a natural barrier to human movement, similar to the seas that surround the Southern half of the African continent. In fact, the southern edge of the Sahara is called the Sahel, an Arabic word which suggests a coast. Still, the Sahara has not been an impenetrable barrier. There were well-established caravan routes across the desert even by the time of the Roman Empire.

The Sahara is a fairly recent geological feature; we believe that what is now the desert was fairly well-watered and generally habitable as recently as around 5,000 B.C.E. (Before the Common Era). Since then, a process of desiccation has resulted in the desert's steady expansion to the north and south. The disastrous droughts in the Sahel in the 1970s, probably exacerbated by environmental mismanagement, forcefully brought this process to the attention of governments and people around the world.

[See Map B]

The escarpments, deserts, and rainforests are all features that have contributed to isolation of human groups within Africa and have served to make contact with people from outside Africa somewhat difficult.

Within the boundaries of Nigeria, most of these geographical features of the continent as a whole are reproduced on a smaller scale. The north is mostly arid country, dry savanna. The Niger River cuts across the country from west to east, taking a sharp turn south when it joins with the Benue River, which flows from east to west from the eastern border of Nigeria. The country is thus divided into two halves: the northern plateaus, semi-arid savanna country, and, below the confluence of the two great rivers, a southern half that is further divided into two parts by the Niger River as it flows to its delta in Southern Nigeria. North of the confluence of the Niger and Benue Rivers is the highest plateau in Nigeria—the Jos Plateau, which was an important site for early iron-working.

To the south, increasing rainfall and vegetation culminate in mostly tropical conditions and dense forests at the coast. The delta of the Niger is the dominant feature of the coast, as the creeks, inlets and mangrove swamps of the delta region stretch from the border with Cameroon nearly to Lagos. Tropical conditions are more pronounced on the eastern side of the Niger, the region roughly associated with the Igbo people. Savanna conditions reach further to the south toward the coast on the western side, the area where the Yoruba people are dominant.

[See Map C]

A further condition that has shaped human life in Africa, and particularly in Nigeria, has been the composition of soils for agriculture. The most prevalent soil on the continent is the mineral type associated with deserts, characterized by minimum fertility (about 28% of the continent is covered by such poor soils). An additional fifth of the soil of Africa is weakly developed or nearly infertile due to lack of moisture or erosion by wind. Almost as much of the soil is high in mineral, particularly iron, content (hence the typical red color of African soils), which is subject to loss of fertility due to leaching by water in areas of high rainfall, such as in the rainforest. Human use of some land has led to further deterioration; for example, in large parts of southern Nigeria, patches of so-called secondary forest are all that remain of what formerly were extensive rainforests.

These conditions of climate, vegetation cover, and soil types are factors contributing to the difficulties of African farmers and food producers in West Africa.

## Food and Agriculture

The geographical features of West Africa resulted in a major division along the lines of food crops, a division represented in Nigeria, as well. In the open savannah of the north, grain or cereal crops could be grown. To the south, in the forest belt, people relied more on root crops, such as yams.

Grains or cereals are actually "ennobled grasses," so it is hardly surprising that as people began to cultivate plants, those living in savannah country would develop the cultivation of grasses. The important cereals have been millet and sorghum. Wild sorghum is indigenous to the African continent, as may be wild millet, although this is less certain. The Ethiopian region of northeast Africa appears to have been an important early area for cultivation of both crops, although a West African cradle for these crops has not been ruled out. There are many different varieties of these grains (for example, in Africa millets include crops known as finger millet and pearl millet). Wild rice, or dry rice (eleusine), was probably developed as a food crop in Ethiopia, as well, but did not become as widespread in West Africa as the sorghums and millets. Cereal crops have been associated with the development of large-scale states in the western Savannah, perhaps because of the scale of organization required for such cultivation and the food surplus thus made possible.

Stretching through the forest belt of West Africa, from the Ivory Coast to the highlands of Cameroon east of Nigeria, runs the area of the Yam Complex. This Yam Complex is nearly coextensive with the distribution of peoples who speak the closely related languages of the Kwa language family (Yoruba and Igbo are both Kwa languages). Interestingly, the yam is not the central food product beyond the area of the Kwa speakers, even though it could have been. Historians assume that yam cultivation began with digging for wild yams and tubers, leading to the practice of gradual cultivation between 2500 and 1500 B.C.E. Other types of yams have been brought to Africa for cultivation, but Igbo traditions make it clear that the indigenous guinea yam is much more prestigious than imported types. In their New Yam Festival, only the traditional yams are used, and these are the only ones that count when designating farmers for honors or titles. These indigenous yams have been fully domesticated; wild yams may still be found in Nigeria and gathered by the very poor for food, but these yams are often toxic and must be pounded and boiled to be made edible.

Other food crops that appear to have been indigenous to Nigeria include cowpeas, a few species of groundnuts (known as peanuts in the U.S.), the oil palm, egusi, (a type of melon), fluted pumpkin, okro (or okra, an example of an Igbo word that has come into English), African breadfruit, Malagueta pepper, and kola nuts, which later became important in long-distance trade in West Africa.

Many important food crops have been borrowed from other continents. These borrowed crops have in many cases become extremely important in the diets and cultures of Africans. The eminent African historian, Jan Vansina, claims, "Cultivation of the banana revolutionized life in the forest."[1] The banana and plantain, water yams, and cocoyams or taro root, all originated in Asia. Botanists agree that the banana reached Africa at least two thousand years ago.

Major crops came also from the Americas, specifically maize (what Americans refer to as corn), cocoa as a major cash crop in modern times, and cassava, also known as manioc. Cassava is quite important in Nigeria today, because the flour of cassava, known as garri, is cheap, filling, and tasty.

Most food animals were borrowed from outside Africa, it appears. Cattle are signs of wealth and well-being throughout Africa. The first variety of cattle in West Africa appear from archaeological records to have been a short-horned, diminutive variety called "muturu" These smaller cattle were later replaced by the larger variety known as "Zebu" cattle, which are humped with long, curving horns. These cattle originated in India. In historical times, Zebu cattle were associated especially with the Fulani people who live throughout the savannah country of West Africa. Herds are not usually found in the forest belt because of lack of grazing land and cattle sickness caused by the tse-tse fly. While the cattle herders such as the Fulani provided butter, milk, and also manure for fertilizer, they also caused some tension because of trampled fields. Even today, cattle are raised primarily for the butter and other dairy goods they produce. In general, Africans do not eat the cattle, except for special occasions or out of necessity. Most of the diets of pastoralists are provided by non-animal, vegetable sources.

**PRINCIPAL CROPS OF MODERN DAY NIGERIAIN ORDER OF PRODUCTION, BY METRIC TON, 1989***

| Crop | Tons |
|---|---|
| Cassava | 15,425 |
| Yams | 9,609 |
| Sorghum | 4,831 |
| Millet | 4,770 |
| Rice (paddy) | 3,303 |
| Maize (corn) | 2,132 |
| Plantains (like bananas) | 1,700 |
| Pulses | 1,456 |
| Other fruits | 1,402 |
| Taro (cocoyam) | 1,299 |
| Sugar cane | 1,180 |
| Groundnuts (peanuts) | 1,017 |
| Palm oi | 857 |
| Palm kernels | 373 |
| Cocoa beans | 160 |

*Latest year with complete data. *Africa South of the Sahara, 1994,* 3rd ed. London: Europa Publications, Ltd., p. 670.

In modern times, many crops have been grown for sale and export rather than for consumption by local peoples. For example, in northern Nigeria today, one sees large fields of cotton and groundnuts for export markets. In the nineteenth century, palm oil became a major export crop from southern Nigeria. Used at first as a lubricant, palm oil is now used primarily for soap and food products. In the western regions of the Nigerian forest belt, cocoa has been developed as an important "cash crop" (for export, rather than for subsistence consumption by the farmers themselves). The table on page 6 clearly shows the continued importance of food crops, especially cassava, but also corn, rice, and yams, to feed Nigeria's huge population. Major cash crops also appear on this list.

## Summary

The physical features of the African continent, such as difficulties of upriver travel, lack of harbors, the barriers of desert, rainforest, and escarpments, have tended to create conditions of isolation from influences outside the continent. On the other hand, the open savannas, as in West Africa, and some of the great rivers, such as the Niger, have allowed for ease of internal travel and migration. The deserts were not impenetrable, moreover, and trade-routes crisscrossed even the great Sahara.

Nigeria exhibits many of the physical features of the rest of the continent, with arid lands and savanna in the North, the great Rivers Niger and Benue in the middle, and the rainforest regions to the South. Many food crops now important in Nigeria were imported from outside Africa, including maize, bananas, and cassava. In the colonial and modern times, there was a drift toward cultivating so-called "cash crops" for export, away from the subsistence agriculture which predominated in earlier times.

## Note

[1] Jan Vansina, "Western Bantu Expansion," *Journal of African History*, 25 (1984), p.141.

# HISTORICAL OVERVIEW OF WEST AFRICA

## Sources for African History

In piecing together the human history of Africa, scholars must rely on a wide range of tools. For most African peoples, the written record begins only within the last few centuries. Other records exist in plenty, however, and provide the primary evidence which is translated by archaeology, linguistics, ethnobotany, and similar sciences into a narrative history of early Africa. Archaeologists study the record of human artifacts, such as remains of dwellings, tools, and weapons; linguists trace the development and diffusion of language; and we have already seen how botanists draw inferences about where and how people live by studying plant population and diffusion. Frequently, two sciences are used in combination. For example, the linguistic root used to denote a particular food or tool can reveal who ate the food or used the tool and where they lived. Archaeology provides a rough dating system for early times. While no historical survey can do justice to the complexities of linguistic and archaeological research, we shall look briefly at some results of such studies in West Africa.

## Language and History in Africa

On the basis of linguistic evidence it appears that the majority of the current population of the southern two-thirds of the African continent settled there "recently," meaning within the last two thousand or so years. There were, of course, people already in these areas before this expansion, probably scattered bands of hunter-gatherers who were absorbed or displaced by the new people, who undoubtedly were farmers.

This great population expansion, the so-called Bantu migrations, is an important theme of early African history. As a linguistic term, "Bantu" denotes a language family, as do the terms "Romance" or "Scandinavian." (In some parts of Africa, particularly southern Africa, "Bantu" when applied to people is an insult.) Many people are familiar with "Romance" languages, which include French, Spanish, Italian, and Romanian. These languages all grew out of Latin, the language of the Romans. After the dissolution of the Roman Empire, the Latin of the Spaniards gradually became distinct from the Latin of the French or the Italians. Eventually, these dialects became mutually unintelligible and were recognized as separate languages. English grew out of the Germanic languages, although the Norman Conquest of England brought French into the linguistic history of English. All these languages grew out of an older parent language in the still more distant past. Linguists today have designated a "family" relationship among a huge number of these languages including English, French, Russian, Persian, Greek, and Hindi. They comprise the Indo-European language family. Most of the other languages of the world similarly can be placed in a few large language families.

Nearly all the languages of Africa can be placed into four large language families, three of them represented in Nigeria. The four major families are:

1. *Afroasiatic,* which includes the Semitic languages of Arabic and Hebrew, as well as the languages of the Berbers of the Sahara Desert, the Amhara of Ethiopia, and the language of the ancient Egyptians, Coptic.

2. *Niger-Kordofanian,* or Niger-Congo, which includes many of the languages of West Africa and the huge sub-family of the Bantu languages.

3. *Nilo-Saharan,* which includes languages spoken by the Maasai of East Africa and by many peoples of the southern Sudan and the Sahelian region of West Africa.

4. *Khoisan,* or Click, which includes the San and Khoi of Southern Africa.

[See Map D. The Languages of Africa.]

The distribution of languages suggests probable routes and times of migrations. The close relatedness and broad dissemination of the Bantu languages suggests that the speakers of these languages expanded over and settled vast areas of the continent quickly and recently, roughly over a time from around 100 to about 1700 C.E. The dark-dashed lines in the white regions of the Niger-Congo languages on the map (Map D) mark major divisions in that huge language family. The Igbo of Nigeria are right at the boundary separating the Kwa Languages of West Africa from the languages of the Bantu branch. Another such line marks the linguistic boundary between the Mande speakers of the early Sudanic empires and the Kwa-speakers, which include the Akan, Yoruba, and Igbo. Regardless of widespread stories concerning migrations of West African peoples from the Middle East or other areas, linguistic evidence indicates that the peoples of West Africa have lived in roughly the same areas for well over two thousand years.

As many as 250 languages are spoken in Nigeria. The Hausa language, spoken over a wide area of northern Nigeria, is of the Afroasiatic branch, which also includes Arabic and Hebrew. The Nigerian people associated with the great early empire of Kanem-Borno, the Kanuri, speak a language of the Saharan branch of the Nilo-Saharan family, which as the map indicates dips all the way down into East Africa and includes peoples such as the Maasai of Kenya and Tanzania. Most of the other peoples of Nigeria speak languages that belong to sub-divisions of the great Niger-Congo family. The Kwa languages are found throughout the forest belt of West Africa, including in Nigeria the Yoruba and Igbo, as well as the Edo, Igala, Nupe, and Ijo. Another major branch of Niger-Congo, called the Benue-Congo sub-family, is closely related to the Bantu family. Speakers of these languages include the Jukun and Tiv of the middle belt region, and the Ekoi, Efik, and lbibio of the southeastern region of Nigeria. The linguistic evidence indicates that the people speaking the West African languages were in or very near their current locations well before the beginning of the great diffusion of Bantu languages into Central, Eastern, and Southern Africa.

## Archaeology and History: Iron Age in Nigeria

The success of the Bantu speakers is thought to derive from their employment of agriculture and iron-working. The population increase associated with these innovations probably occurred before

1000, and even earlier for iron age peoples of West Africa (dates without B.C.E. are to be understood as belonging to the Common Era, or A.D. by the traditional dating system).

Archaeologists have dated iron-working at the area of Taruga in central Nigeria to the sixth or seventh century B.C.E. and in the Nok culture in northern Nigeria to 300 B.C.E. In addition to the signs of iron-working, terra cotta—or earthenware—masks were discovered in 1936 and 1944 on the Jos Plateau near the modern town of Nok. Since 1944 many more Nok terra cottas have been discovered, some of high artistic merit. The art of the Nok people appears to be of great antiquity and is thought to foreshadow the artistic traditions of the Yoruba.

The presence of early iron-working in these areas of Nigeria suggests that the knowledge of iron-smelting and smithing reached Africa by one or both of two routes: from the Nile River region west across the savannahs, and/or from the ancient state of Carthage on the North African coast south across the early trade routes. People who had mastered iron production had several advantages over populations still using stone implements. Iron tools allowed for much more productive farming, and iron weapons were more effective in protecting farm land, as well as people, from predators. Iron-working thus led to a more rapid build-up of population and to a settled way of life in a society more highly organized than had been possible earlier.

## The Sudanic Kingdoms of West Africa

The African past is a culturally rich one. Traditional societies, however organized, all had developed systems of community—systems of governance and of defense, labor, economics, architecture, art, religion, and kinship. The period of the great kingdoms of West Africa stretches over more than ten centuries, the earliest arising about 800 and the latest reaching their height by 1400. These kingdoms were of two primary types: the earlier were the northern Sudanic kingdoms, which arose on the fringes of the Sahara Desert and grew rich and powerful through trans-Saharan trade in gold, salt, and textiles; the more southerly were the kingdoms of the forest, some developing as terminus points for Saharan trade (and as sources for gold, kola nuts, and other trade commodities) and others in response to the rise of Atlantic trade in slaves, weapons, and manufactured goods. A third type of socio-political organization of particular importance to our study is the small-scale or "stateless" society characteristic of the Igbo of southeastern Nigeria.

## Ghana, Mali, and Songhai

As early as the 700s Arabic documents report a great empire to the south of the Sahara Desert deriving its prosperity and power from trans-Saharan trade in gold and salt. The Ghana, or ruler, of the empire which became known to history as the great state of Ghana, was the traditional head of a West African people known as the Soninke. As the Soninke gained control of the southern termini of the gold-salt trade, they were able to extend their power over neighboring peoples. Militarily, this power was probably based on horses, acquired in trade and used for cavalry. In the open savannah country, cavalry provided for swift movement and communication conducive to larger political organization. Ghana is now recognized as the first of a series of entities collectively known as the Sudanic Kingdoms of West Africa. "Sudan" comes from the Arabic for "Land of the Black Peoples" and refers to the vast open land of the savannahs sweeping from the coast of Senegal through the area drained by the Niger River to the region of Lake Chad and on to the area of the modern Republic of the Sudan.

Two more great empires, Mali and Songhai, successively replaced early Ghana as the powers controlling the gold and salt trade of the western Sudan. There was a long break between the fall of Ghana and the rise of Mali. For a time, no single ethnic group succeeded in gaining control of the trade network. In 1230, however, a great leader of the Mandinke peoples appeared: Sundiata Keita (or Sunjata).

Sundiata, who based his power on the creation of what we would call a standing army, established control over the gold-producing regions as well as the area of the great bend of the Niger River, taking the title of Mansa, or lord. His great rival, whom he defeated in a climactic battle was identified as both a blacksmith and a "magician," which probably means that Sundiata's success marked the victory of Islam over rulers who based their authority on more traditional belief systems.

His military sovereignty assured, Sundiata turned his attention to domestic matters—to caravan trade and the cultivation of crops and grains, including cotton. Thus did the Empire of Mali grow rich and Sundiata's fame increase. His story, first set down in an ancient Arabic manuscript, lives on in the stories and dances of West Africa.

Sundiata appears to have been only a nominal Muslim, remaining a hero of traditional religion as well as representing the coming of Islam. His successors, however, were more thoroughly Muslim. The most powerful of these was Mansa Musa, whose spectacular pilgrimage to Mecca in 1324 included an entourage of 8,000 people in a year-long journey of some 9,000 miles. Working from the accounts of Muslim scribes, Lester Brooks writes:

> Certainly the emperor's trip was the sensation of the Moslem world. It literally put Mali on the map. Maps of Africa after this time almost always show Mali and many have drawings of Mansa Musa. They usually show him as a black emperor with robe, crown, scepter and orb of gold. Mali became fixed in people's minds as the Eldorado—country with limitless gold, and as a result there was an even greater flow of traders, merchants, religious leaders and scholars to the empire.[1]

Mansa Musa returned to the Western Sudan with Muslim scholars from the Middle East, and subsequently built great mosques at Gao and Timbuctu on the Niger River. These cities became important Muslim centers. The famous Muslim traveler, Ibn Batutta from Morocco, visited Mali during the reign of Mansa Musa's successor and found it to be a secure and prosperous kingdom.

As Mali's prosperity declined toward the end of the fourteenth century, a new state rose to preeminence: Songhai. Early traditions place the founding of the Songhai state in the seventh century along the Niger River. Around 1300, new rulers with the title of Sunni or Shi appeared among the Songhai. The greatest of these rulers was Sunni Ali, the hero of the expansion of the empire, including his conquest of the famous city of Timbuctu in the heart of the older Mali Empire. Like Sundiata, Sunni Ali appears to have been a nominal Muslim, who may even have persecuted some of the Muslim clerics of Timbuctu. Perhaps for this reason, he had a poor reputation among the Islamic scholars, who may have plotted against him even during his lifetime. Such plotting led to the overthrow of Sunni Ali's son and successor and the establishment of a new powerful, strictly Islamic dynasty, that of the Askias. This new ruler was Askia Muhammed the

Great, who became the Khalifa (Caliph or Deputy) of the Western Sudan following his Hajj to Mecca in 1496 or 1497. He is known to have led a jihad, or Muslim holy war, against some other African states south of the Niger River. The Empire of Songhai reached its greatest extent (and the greatest extent of any of the great West African empires) during the great Askia's reign, extending certainly into the area of the Hausa people in Northern Nigeria.

The history of these states show the increasing power and influence of Islam as we move from the time of Ghana up to the period of the great empire of Songhai. The coup of the Askias in that empire reveal the political role that Muslim clerics could play in the largest of the African states of that time.

[See Map E. States of West Africa]

## Kanem-Borno

Around the shores of Lake Chad, another powerful Sudanic African empire developed: the state now known as Kanem-Borno. Arabic sources refer to a state of Kanem as early as 872. The Kanembu people established a hegemony over the trade routes in the central Sudanic area in the ninth century in the area called Kanem, to the east of Lake Chad. These trade routes ran from Lake Chad north to the shores of Libya and east across the savannahs to the Nile, providing a link with Egypt and the Middle East. By the 1000s, a divine king, known as the Mai, was ruling in Kanem. A Muslim gained control of the state and became the Mai sometime between 1075 and 1085. This man, known as Hummay or Umme, established the dynasty known as the Saifwa. This name is taken from that of an early Muslim hero, probably in an attempt to reinforce the family's Islamic links. Linguistic evidence indicates that the Kanembu and other African peoples of the region did not come from the Middle East but had been in or near their present location for many centuries. By the 1100s, there are reports of a Mai making at least two pilgimages to Mecca, establishing more links with the Middle East. Despite the national conversion to Islam, certain non-Islamic practices, such as secluding the Mai from the gaze of the people, were retained until well into the nineteenth century.

The early Kanem empire reached the height of its power in the thirteenth century. By the middle of that century, the Mais had extended their influence into what is today southern Libya and west as far as the Hausa state of Kano. Diplomatic relations were established with Tunisia on the Mediterranean coast. The economic base of the state was trade in slaves; Kanem was too far East to have access to the gold that fueled the trade of Ghana, Mali, and Songhai. Following this brief period of expansion, Kanem fell into a period of anarchy and internal strife, leading the dynasty to re-locate across Lake Chad in the Borno region of modern-day Nigeria, hence the identification of the empire later as Kanem-Borno. The dominant Kanembu people were displaced by a new people, called the Kanuri, who probably developed from a combination of Kanembu and other African peoples in the area. Stability was established around 1470 and a new walled capital called Gazarngamu was constructed.

The state then embarked on a second period of expansion; the old region of Kanem was re-occupied and a flourishing trade with Egypt developed. The most famous and powerful of all the Mais came to power in 1569 or 1570; this ruler was Mai ldris Alooma, who, like Askia Muhammed, inherited the title of Khalifa, a Muslim title for a representative of the successor of the prophet.[2] This Mai established direct diplomatic relations with the Turkish capital of Istanbul and launched several jihads against neighboring states and people. One such jihad took him to the gates of the Hausa city of Kano, which he besieged. Clearly, Muslim clerics and teachers (the ulama) became extremely influential during the reign of Mai Idris Alooma.

The Islamic Kanuri people of northeastern Nigeria remain one of the most important ethnic groups in Northern Nigeria today. The writer, Zaynab Alkali, for example, is a member of this ethnic group. *The Stillborn,* her novel of life during the colonial period of Nigeria, reveals that even after long centuries of Islamic influence there were still vestiges of ancestral religion in the rural areas of Borno. The grandmother of the novel's central character is clearly a practitioner of the older faith, while the younger generation are probably only nominal Muslims. The novelist suggests that Islam has had more influence in urban rather than rural areas over the years.

## Hausa States

The western half of northern Nigeria came to be dominated by the ethnic group called the Hausa, whose language belongs to the Chadic branch of the Afroasiatic family. The Hausa developed a number of small but powerful city-states that participated in the

Sudanic trading networks. Located between the areas dominated by Mali and Songhai on the one side and Kanem-Borno on the other, Hausa cities were nearly always dominated by one or the other of the great empires.

The Hausa cities were founded sometime around 1000. Traditions suggest that the founding hero was a "King of Baghdad" who came to the area, killed a giant snake that blocked people's access to water, and married a local queen of the town of Daura. This king's son had six sons, who in turn became the first kings of Daura, Kano, Zaria, Gobir, Katsina, and Rano; the son of a daughter became the king of a smaller Hausa city. These became the original seven Hausa *Bakwai*, or states. Of the seven, only four had a significant impact on West African history: Kano, Katsina, Zaria, and Gobir.

Founding myths of this sort are not unusual in Africa. They may refer to vaguely remembered events—such as a small group of newcomers establishing their rule through conquest and marriage. The linguistic evidence, however, indicates that the Hausa people have been in their current location for a very long time, calling into question the historical reality of their migrating from the East or elsewhere. Traditions of this sort may rather represent an effort to legitimize political claims based on Islamic heroes or traditions.

The Hausa were early town-dwellers, setting them apart from most African peoples, who lived in villages or small family-based compounds. Towns were located near sources of iron ore and on defensible sites. Towns that gave access to trade routes became important local trade centers for surrounding farmers. In fact, trade may have been the most important factor in the concentration of people in such towns. These towns grew into walled cities, becoming known as "*Birnin* Kano" or "*Birnin* Katsina," meaning "walled Kano" and "walled Katsina." Eventually, locally manufactured leather became a major item in trans-Saharan trade. "Moroccan" leather, in fact, came from the Hausa of northern Nigeria; it was called "Moroccan" because the usual European point of purchase was Morocco.

Islam came into the Hausa states with traders from Mali and Kanem-Borno. Mandinke traders from Mali, known as either the *Dyula* or the *Wangara*, were especially influential in the spreading of Islam into Hausaland and other parts of West Africa. Tradition maintains that the eleventh ruler of Kano went over to Islam between

1350 and 1385. In the 1400s, Muhammed Rumfa, the *Sarki* (ruler) of Kano, was known as a staunch Muslim. He sought the advice of an important Muslim cleric, al-Maghili, who wrote for Muhammed Rumfa the book *The Obligation of Princes. The Chronicle of Kano,* written by Muslim scholars, praises this Hausa ruler as a builder of mosques and enforcer of Muslim law.

## Early Forest Kingdoms of West Africa

South of the great bend of the Niger River, the traders from the Sudanic belt, the Dyula or Wangara mentioned above, sought to organize the peoples of the forests to facilitate trading. The largest states or kingdoms were developed in the following areas: the vicinity of modern Ghana, Ivory Coast, and Togo—the so-called Akan states; the region of southwestern Nigeria—the area of the Yoruba and Edo peoples; and an area directly west of Nigeria, among speakers of the Fon language, traditionally the state of Dahomey (but on the modern map, the Republic of Benin).

In addition to gold from the Akan areas, an important item of trade was the kola nut, which grows in the tropical regions from the modern Ivory Coast through Southern Nigeria. The kola trade is possibly very ancient. In the West of the region, the trade was dominated by Akan-speakers and Mandinke Dyula traders from Mali or Songhai. The people of Oyo and the Hausa came to dominate the kola trade further East in the region of modern Nigeria. The Hausa traders also became quite important in the East-West trade in kolas running from the Volta River region of the Akan people to Hausaland. The long-distance trade required considerable skill and organization, because the nuts, if allowed to dry out, lost their value, taste, and texture. In novels of Chinua Achebe, especially the classic *Things Fall Apart,* the kola nut is shown to be an important part of traditional Igbo hospitality. The Muslim traders from the North valued it as one of the few stimulants not prohibited by the Koran. The high caffeine content kept caravan traders awake and alert during their long journeys. Kola eventually became a key ingredient, obviously, in American soft drinks.

## The Akan States

Akan languages are spoken throughout the area of modern Ghana and the Ivory Coast. The Akan states were smaller than were the Sudanic kingdoms because the dense vegetation and the tse-tse flies of the forest prevented the use of cavalry. Although the areas were small, the populations were denser than in the Sudanic belt.

In the 1480s Europeans appeared at the coast of West Africa, learned of alluvial gold deposits and named the area of the Akan peoples "The Gold Coast." These newcomers represented a new and much greater opportunity for trade than had the Muslims from the north, so there was a reorientation from desert north to the Atlantic south. By 1750, most of the Akan states had been absorbed by two rival kingdoms: the Ashanti (or Asante) in the central part of modern-day Ghana, and the Fanti near the coast, both seeking access to the lucrative Atlantic trade. Eventually, the Ashanti kingdom became dominant—powerful enough to fight several wars with the British in the 1800s. By that time, Hausa traders from the area of Nigeria had established themselves in trading compounds in parts of the Akan-speaking area, even in the capital of the Ashanti empire.

## Oyo and Benin

The pattern of the Akan states was repeated to the East in the region of southwestern Nigeria. Although for convenience we refer to the kingdoms in this area as "forest" kingdoms, in fact the dense forest was broken in the area in which the great empire of Oyo developed. Oyo consequently had many features in common with the Sudanic kingdoms, such as dependence upon cavalry for their military might.

The largest empires in this area of Nigeria were formed by the Yoruba and Edo peoples. Both groups traditionally trace their history to the ancient Yoruba city of Ife, which was a spiritual center for both the Yoruba and Edo in historic times. Radiocarbon dates at archaeological digs showing remains of glass works suggest that Ife became a settlement of considerable size between the ninth and twelfth centuries. The impressive bronze sculptures of Ife indicate a trading link with the Sudanic belt, which would have supplied the necessary copper.

The founder of the city of Ife was said to be Oduduwa (or Obatala), one of the Yoruba *orishas*, or deities. Oduduwa descended from heaven on a golden chain, sprinkling sand from a sack to make dry land appear on the surface of the vast waters. A rooster, which he had also brought from heaven, scratched and scattered the land into hills, valleys, and islands. Then Oduduwa jumped down, landing on the spot that became Ife, the center of the earth, there to reign as the first *Oni*, or ruler, of Ife. The name of the city, *Ile Ife*, can be translated as "original home of that which is wide," or origin of the earth (*Ile* means original or original home). Traditional belief is that a son or grandson of Oduduwa, known as Oranmiyan or Oranyan, sent sons from Ife to found the royal dynasties of the various Yoruba kingdoms and the Benin kingdom of the related Edo people.[3] The general word for chief or ruler at any level among the Yoruba is "oba," but specific obas generally have titles that include the name of the city or state over which they rule. Oni is hence probably a shortened version of Onife (ruler of Ife).

Oyo became one of the most powerful of African empires. Radiocarbon dates indicate a settlement there as early as 1100, with a sizable urban population by 1400. Oyo is sometimes translated from Yoruba as "slippery place," because the horse of Oranyan is said to have slipped on the ground on the side of the hill that became the original site of Oyo (*Oyo Ile*, "original Oyo"). Although some traditions trace the founding of the city back to Oranyan, the son of Oduduwa, Shango was the legendary founder in other myths. In some versions, Shango was a son or grandson of Oduduwa and a prince from the neighboring kingdom of Nupe, north of Oyo. Such traditions suggest a connection between the ruling families of Ife and Nupe in the founding of Oyo. Oyo reached its zenith during the seventeenth and eighteenth centuries. During that time, Oyo dominated all the peoples in the open country down to the coast. The ruler, or oba, of Oyo took the title, Alafin, which means ruler of the "palace," which in Yoruba is "afin."

Oyo's expansion into an empire no doubt owes its inception to involvement in the long-distance trans-Saharan trade. Like Ife and even Benin, it was conveniently located both for defense and as a trade terminus. As was the case with the Akan states, however, the appearance of new traders on the ocean—the Europeans—provided a new impetus for expanding control over trade routes. Indeed, the greatest power of Oyo followed contact with European trade and probably derives from the prosperity such contact made possible.

This trade eventually was dominated by slavery as the Europeans sought to provide cheap labor for sugar plantations in the New World. Oyo and other African trading kingdoms became enmeshed in the Atlantic slave trade, as we will see in a later section of this text. Power increasingly was based on access to the guns and other European products the slave trade provided. The coast of the area of Dahomey, subordinate to the Oyo empire nearly into the nineteenth century, was called the "Slave Coast" by the European sailors.

Oyo[4] was by far the largest and most powerful of the Yoruba states, covering perhaps 10,000 square miles. It and the other Yoruba states are discussed further in the next chapter. Benin, although small in area because of its location in dense forest, was also powerful, and home to an artistic tradition of world importance—the famous Benin bronzes. Some art historians see similarity between these bronze sculptures and the terra cotta heads of the ancient Nok culture. The kingdom of Benin was founded by the Edo people, whose language is quite similar to those of the Yoruba and Igbo, their western and eastern neighbors, respectively.

The foundations of Benin are unclear. An Oba succeeded in becoming paramount over other village leaders and chiefs sometime around 1200–1300. According to legend, the Edo people sent to Oduduwa at Ife, asking for a king to rule over them. Historically, these traditions indicate a connection through Ife between Yoruba and Edo traditions. Possibly in a secession crisis or other local dispute, the Edo sent to Ife for a compromise ruler, or the tradition may indicate a conquest of the area of Benin by leaders from Ife, with the story added later about their having been invited to rule.

Having succeeded in enhancing his power at the expense of the council of nobles, the fourth Oba renamed the state Ubini (or Benin). Thereafter the people of this kingdom are often referred to as Bini rather than the more general term, Edo. Members of this ruling dynasty are credited with the introduction of brass casting from Ife, new kinds of weapons, and horses. The wealth necessary to support Benin's elaborate art and court traditions probably came from its trans-Saharan trading interests.

An Oba named Ewuare, remembered as the greatest ruler of Benin, embarked on a series of conquests that made Benin into an empire in the 1400s. He extended control over some Igbo as well as some of the eastern Yoruba states. Art flourished at Benin in this period (1504–1550), a sort of "colony" was established at Lagos, and the first contact was made with Europeans at the coast. (Lagos was called Eko by the Yoruba, hence the traditional ruler of the city was the Eleko. Lagos derives from the Portuguese name for the area, Lago de Curamo). The Portuguese established diplomatic relations with Benin, and Bini ambassadors were dispatched to Lisbon, Rome, and some other European cities. Trade was reoriented toward the Atlantic rather than the north, and the slave trade became important.

## Small-Scale Societies of Southern Nigeria

In many parts of Africa, people were not organized into large-scale states or kingdoms. European administrators during the colonial period referred to these small-scale societies as "stateless." Scholars today contend that the distinction between African states and "stateless" peoples is somewhat misleading. Most Africans found their lives to be organized quite similarly whether they were technically subjects of an empire, such as Mali or Oyo, or were residents of "stateless" societies as were the Igbo of Nigeria. Everyday life took place largely within the village and its near environs, while outward-directed pursuits such as trade or warfare were sporadic or temporary. People in small-scale polities lived ordered lives within the regulated system so neatly detailed in Achebe's *Things Fall Apart*. Some estimates place the number of small-scale societies among the Igbo at 2,700.

Along the coast of the Atlantic small communities of various ethnic groups were located on the creeks, inlets, and lagoons of the delta country where the people lived by fishing and gathering salt. These small communities were in a good position to take advantage of trading opportunities when the European ships appeared off the coast in the fifteenth and sixteenth centuries. Some grew into small trading cities engaged in the Atlantic slave trade and, later, in the palm oil trade with the Europeans. The cities were dominated by large trading "houses" managed by the heads of important families with their retainers, supporters, and slaves. In each city three or four such houses organized the trade with English, French, Portuguese, and other European traders. Secret societies provided connections among the leaders and traders of the houses in the various cities and towns of the coast. These secret societies, with rituals of initiation and festivals, provided links among the houses and cities that allowed for coordination among the Africans in their dealings with the Europeans.

## The Igbo

The people of the hinterland constituted one of the largest ethnic groups in Nigeria (and in Africa, for that matter): the Igbo. The Igbo, whose language is part of the large Kwa sub-family of West Africa, are located at the eastern edge of the Kwa-speaking group. Like the other Kwa speakers, the Igbo are part of the Yam Complex, indicating an affinity with other West African peoples of the coastal region of West Africa.

Igbo are found on both sides of the Niger River, although the majority are on the eastern side. Those on the western side, probably influenced by Benin and similar kingdoms, did establish some large-scale states or kingdoms. On the eastern side, however, small-scale, village-based societies predominate. The Igbo have one of the densest rural populations in Africa, almost 1,000 people to the square mile. Archaeological finds of pottery from 5,000 years ago resemble pottery made by modern Igbo. Such artifacts, together with linguistic evidence, suggest that the Igbo are a very ancient people in southeastern Nigeria. The Igbo were making widespread use of iron tools by the first century. Major growth and expansion of the Igbo population seems to have occurred from the ninth century onwards, as they gradually spread out from a central core area over the region that they occupy today.

## Summary

Our brief historical overview of the context in which the cultures of West Africa developed clearly points to a high level of social, political, and artistic sophistication in existence long before the coming of the Europeans. The most important catalyst for further development was probably international trade, beginning with the long-distance caravan trade in the north which brought to Nigeria an international religion, Islam. With Islam came a writing script, Arabic, and Islamic patterns of social and political organization, particularly among the Hausa and the Kanuri of Kanem-Borno. In southern Nigeria, the international trade route shifted orientation from the Sudanic North to the Atlantic, along which eventually traveled not only goods and slaves but new ideas, as well. The peoples of the forest, or Guinea, region developed both centralized states and small-scale, village-based societies. The area of the Kwa-speaking people, encompassing the area of the "Yam Complex," stretched from the Akan areas in the West to the Yoruba, Edo, and Igbo peoples in Nigeria. The Hausa traders eventually established themselves as far afield as the Akan empire of Ashanti. The Yoruba and Edo, traditionally town dwellers, organized some of the more powerful centralized kingdoms of West Africa, notably the empires of Oyo and Benin. Most of the Igbo, despite their dense population, did not develop monarchies, police, or military forces, nor even traditions or histories standard throughout all Igbo areas. Clearly, ethnic and linguistic similarity do not necessarily lead to similar political and social structures.

## Notes

1 *Great Civilizations of Ancient Africa,* New York: Four Winds Press, 1971, page 137.

2 "*Alooma*" (pronounced "ah-lome-ah") was actually applied to his name after his death in a battle in a swamp called "*Aloo.*"

3 The seven sons of Oduduwa, sent out from Ife according to legend, became the Oba of Benin, the Olowa of Owu, the Orangun of Ila, the Alafin of Oyo, the Onisabe of Sabe, the Olupopo of Popo, and the Alaketu of Ketu.

4 A list of some of the other Yoruba states in the forest belt will indicate the complexity of the actual situation: Ijebu, to the south of Oyo; Owu, which was often subordinate to Oyo; Owo, which was often in the Benin sphere of influence; Ilorin, in the north, was eventually part of the Muslim Fulani empire; Ondo, which refers to "settlers" from the Oduduwa tradition; and the Ijesha state. Abeokuta was founded by the Egba branch of Yoruba in the Nineteenth Century as the old Oyo empire fell apart. The powerful kingdom of Ibadan had similar origins in the 1800s.

# TRADITIONAL SOCIETIES OF NIGERIA

One cannot yet speak of a "Nigerian" culture or national identity. There are as many as 250 different ethnic cultures within the boundaries of the modern Republic of Nigeria. Still, three ethnic groups have become dominant in each of three geographical areas of the country—the Hausa in the north, the Yoruba in the southwest, and the Igbo in the southeast. Today, these three peoples represent some of the largest ethnic groups in all of Africa. The focus of this text is consequently on the traditions of these three groups. Remember, however, that these ethnic identifications are relatively recent themselves. Many people now designated Hausa, for example, may not traditionally have thought of themselves in those terms.

Although we know more about the history of the Hausa and the Yoruba than about that of the Igbo, recent anthropological study provides us with significant information concerning the traditional way of life among the Igbo as well as the other two peoples. Although the traditions described here are presented as aspects of the historical past, the reader should bear in mind that African tradition remains vital in the modern world.

## The Importance of Kinship

These three peoples, like many other African groups, placed great importance on kinship in organizing their societies. Lines of kinship were used for establishing one's identity, role, and obligations within the community. Two features of kinship organization are particularly important in understanding how these systems worked. The first is the principle of unilineal descent. Americans have some difficulty in identifying ancestors back through very many generations because we trace descent through both parents—so we have four grandparents, eight great-grandparents, sixteen great great-grandparents, and so on. In a system of unilineal descent, ancestors are traced only through fathers or mothers, not both—so one would have two grandparents, two great-grandparents, and so on. The second feature was a consequence of the widespread practice of polygyny, which resulted in many half-brothers and half-sisters who were, however, related through the lineage (the people tracing descent from a common ancestor through unilineal descent).

Several lineages could be related to some more distant ancestor, which resulted in an identification sometimes called a clan, although this term tends to be loosely applied. "Tribe," or ethnic group, is an amalgamation of all the lineages and clans sharing a common language, culture and, often, religious beliefs and practices.

Africans are and have been overwhelmingly rural, living in farming communities or compounds. Typically, the household comprises a man and one or several wives, their children, other relatives, such as grandparents, aunts, or uncles, and clients—people who for one reason or another are not attached to a specific family group. In some areas in past times, there also would have been clients who could be described as slaves associated with the family compound (war captives, hostages, ritually-designated slaves, purchased slaves, or others). Family relationships, then, tended to be more complex than is the case with the smaller, nuclear families now associated with American living styles.

An individual was therefore identified as a member of several kinship groups—a family, a lineage, perhaps a clan. In addition, other groups provided identity and demanded some allegiance or loyalty. For example, young people of approximately the same age from a particular area, lineage, or ethnic group might be thought of as constituting one such identifiable group. Often, these young people underwent a period of instruction and initiation together, which resulted in their developing a special loyalty to each other across kinship lines. Other age groups were possible bases for identification, as well. For a particular set of years, a man was a warrior, then a junior elder, then a senior elder, and so on.

Marriage outside one's own lineage or clan (exogamy) also resulted in in-law obligations and loyalties that cut across direct kinship lines. Exogamy was often required; marriage to a "relative" within the lineage was not permitted.

People in African cultures may be thought of as both belonging in and belonging to specified kinship groups. "Belonging to" implies that the group had some authority over that individual and that he or she owed definite obligations to the group. An individual without such ties would be considered an outsider or stranger, with no rights and with no protection. Describing his own people, Victor Uchendu writes that an Igbo without a patrilineage "is an Igbo without citizenship."[1] Traditionally, an African had rights and freedoms only as part of a body or community. American notions of individualism would seem strange and unfamiliar in these contexts.

[See Map F. Major Ethnic Groups of Nigeria.]

The map of major cultural groups in Nigeria (Map F) reveals the ethnic complexity of that country, although this map shows only the larger groups. There are many smaller, distinct peoples as well. The three largest groups, which serve as the foci of this text, do not comprise the entire modern nation, a point which can easily be forgotten when thinking of Nigeria's ethnic problems of today. The 'F' on the map represents the presence of the pastoral Fulani people, who follow their herds through lands otherwise occupied by other ethnic groups. This text has already alluded to other important ethnic groups as well: the Kanuni in the northeast, the Edo of the Benin Empire in southern Nigeria, the Nupe, who may have been involved in the founding of the early dynasty of Oyo, and the coastal peoples such as the Ijo and lbibio located between the Igbo and the Atlantic. As the table on the following page reveals, the three largest groups today comprise almost two-thirds of the population of Nigeria; the ten largest groups account for fully 80%. Together with closely related peoples, these ethnic groups total over 93% of the nation's population.

## The Hausa

Authorities question whether there is or has been a uniform Hausa cultural identity. The term seems to refer more to a collection of peoples speaking the Hausa language, while exhibiting many variations in life style, world view, and value system. Hausa has become a lingua franca in use throughout a wide area of the West African savannah. Some estimates place the number of Hausa speakers today as high as 38 million, 32 million in northern Nigeria alone. Most other Hausa today live in the Republic of Niger north of Nigeria, artificially separated from Nigeria's Hausa by the borders the British and French drew to demarcate their respective spheres of influence during the colonial period. The Hausa language, which uses a form of Arabic script known as *ajami,* provided a written literature in this part of West Africa long before European influences reached the region. The impact of modern institutions and political life have served to mold a Hausa culture more uniform today than that which probably existed in earlier history.

**TABLE 1. PEOPLES OF NIGERIA THE LARGEST OF 250 IDENTIFIABLE ETHNIC GROUPS**

| Ethnic Group | % of Population | Cumulative % |
|---|---|---|
| Hausa-Fulani | 29% | 29% |
| Yoruba | 20% | 49% |
| Igbo | 17% | 66% |
| Tiv and Plateau groups | 9% | |
| lbibio, Efik and related groups | 6% | |
| Kanuri | 5% | |
| Edo | 3% | |
| Idoma, Igala, Igbirra | 2.5% | |
| Ijo,or Ijaw | 2% | 93% |

Source: Morrison, Donald G., Robert Cameron Mitchell, John Naber Paden, Hugh Michael Stevenson, *Black Africa: A Comparative Handbook,* New York: The Free Press, 1979, p. 311; Moroney, Sean (Ed.) *Africa: Vol. 1. Handbooks to the Modern World,* New York: Facts on File Publications, 1989, pp. 403–404.

The Hausa have long identified closely with the Islamic religion, which came to Hausaland in the fourteenth century. Historically, the Hausa have adhered to the Sunni branch of Islam and followed the Maliki school of law. Islam brought the Hausa in touch with an international civilization with an institutionalized legal system, writing, literature, and architecture. Hausa children typically studied in Koranic schools with a *mallam* (boys still receive much more such education than girls). The mallams often dispensed protective medicines or charms, as well. For example, the water used to wash a Koranic sura from a board was thought to have talismanic effects. The mallams were maintained by *zakat* (charity), as required by Islam, but many of them had small farms, too.

As in the present day, men in Hausa communities of the past often belonged to one of the Muslim brotherhoods, or *tariqas*, the most important of which among the Hausa is still the *Tijaniyya*. Large numbers of Hausa have performed the hajj (in fact, the central government organizes airline flights to Mecca and Medina for this purpose today). The Hausa traditionally practiced some forms of female exclusion, although women were free to visit each other in the evenings and to visit relatives. They even carried on trade through the use of intermediaries.

The effects of the Islamic influence were far-reaching for the Hausa. They were brought into contact with a world history and tradition. The literacy brought by Arabic script allowed for the development of a written literature, record-keeping for a bureaucracy as well as for business dealings, and an external, international set of values carried through the *Qu'ran*, the *shari'a* (the system of Islamic law), and the Muslim scholars and clerics. The Islamic presence also set up a continuing, often unresolved tension between the traditional beliefs and values of the Hausa polities and the newer, occasionally intolerant and militant values of the Muslim community. Movements of Islamic reform and fundamentalism, such as the Fulani jihads of the nineteenth century, often threatened to undermine the power of traditional Hausa rulers, even though they were themselves Muslims.

The economic base for each Hausa state depended upon factors such as location and history. For example, Gobir, as the northernmost of the states, was very much involved in the trans-Saharan trade through relationships with Songhai and Kanem-Borno, as well as with the Tuareg Berbers of the north. Kano and Katsina were more involved with the trade organized from the Mali and Songhai regions to their West. This long-distance and medium-distance trade took Hausa traders south to the Benue River region, East to Borno, and West as far as the Volta River region of the Akan-speakers. While the trade across the Sahara was carried on by use of camels, this southern trade along the fringes of the forest depended upon the donkey, oxen, and human porters. The Hausa were also adept at the canoe-borne trade on the Niger River. This involvement in trade led to the important profession of the *maduga*, or the caravan-leader among the Hausa. Historians speak of a Hausa "diaspora," or dispersion, as Hausa traders established camps, called *zongos*, as far West as the Ashanti empire in modern-day Ghana.

Throughout historical times, the Hausa were divided among several social classes. At the top of the hierarchy were the ruling class, made up of the "chiefs," or *Sarakuna* (singular, *Sarki*) and courtiers. The Muslim *ulama* (scholars, judges, teachers) and wealthy merchants were politically and socially prominent. Then there were the urban populations of the towns and cities, both free and slave, and the people of the countryside who were both free peasants and agricultural slaves, some of whom lived in slave villages or worked on large farms owned by *Sarakuna*, courtiers, or wealthy merchants. On the margins of the Hausa society were the pastoral nomads living in Fulani cattle encampments. Most of the members of the ruling class considered themselves Muslims. Town dwellers included craftsmen, shopkeepers, small merchants, and the like, as well as some beggars and the poor (in Islamic countries, beggars are not necessarily poor; in Kano, some were reciters of poems and songs who received fairly good incomes from alms).

In the rural areas, essentially the entire adult male population is still today engaged in farming as the primary occupation, particularly cultivating sorghum and millet for food. Low average population density allows for generally widespread access to adequate farm land. The work is very labor intensive, since most work is done with the hoe as the only tool or machinery. Ox-drawn plows are fairly rare, and tractors rarer still. Each rural family lives in a compound, called a *gida* in Hausa, with a compound head, normally the oldest adult male. Men primarily are responsible for field work, while women's primary duties lie in child-rearing, housework, threshing and grinding grain, and cooking. The growing acceptance of the Islamic practice of *purdah* (secluding women) further restricts women's occupation outside the home.[2]

Marriage is nearly universal and virtually obligatory. Roles for single persons, such as bachelor, nun, or unmarried priest, simply do not exist. Pressure is exerted on women, particularly, to marry quite young and to stay married throughout their fertile years. Over half the women are married by age 14 and nearly 100% are married by age 19. Young widows and divorcees are seen as having a duty to get remarried, or they risk being perceived as prostitutes.[3] Men are under intense pressure to marry, as well, but not at such a young age. As in many parts of Nigeria, and Africa in general, marriage is a public, family matter, not a private arrangement between two individuals. Bridewealth constitutes the visible or tangible sign of the contractual obligations marriage creates between two family groups or compounds. Polygamy is acceptable and even encouraged given the pressure on women to be married and the typical surplus of women of marriageable age over the number of available adult males.

Historically, in both towns and rural areas, there were different categories of slaves, reminding us that in non-Western countries the concept of slavery is much more complex than in American experience. For example, some were born into their status but were servants of powerful chiefs and kings and could themselves wield considerable influence. One of the early Kings or Mansas of Mali, Sakura, began his career as such a slave. There were house slaves, essentially domestic servants, who were often considered nearly members of the family. In the countryside were the inhabitants of so-called slave villages, who worked for absentee farm-owners, but also had the right to own and work their own farm plots as well. Some scholars have suggested their status was more like that of the serfs of Russia rather than of slaves. Usually these kinds of slaves were not those transported across the Sahara in the slave trade. This trade appears to have depended upon war captives or others captured in raids on surrounding peoples.

In Kano, crafts were particularly important, such as cloth weaving and, later, cloth dyeing and leather working. Still, most Hausa were farmers, often living within the walls of the towns or cities and going out to till their fields in the day. Living within the area of the "Cereal Complex," they cultivated millet and sorghum as primary grain crops, using the hoe as the basic tool. Farmers did not make use of draft animals for plowing or cultivating. During long dry seasons, the farmers often turned to crafts for supplemental income. In modern times, they have added cultivation of cash crops, such as groundnuts (peanuts) and cotton.

While there were rivalries among the various states, no one of them was able to subdue the others, so there was no overarching Hausa Empire. As wealth from long-distance trade became more important, however, intra-Hausa rivalry appears to have been exacerbated. As warfare spread among the states, taxation increased, as did the growing separation between the Hausa elite and the common people. These changes provide an important background to the revolutions that spread throughout Hausaland in the nineteenth century as a result of the Fulani jihads, or holy wars.

The association between Hausa and Fulani became so close in northern Nigeria in the nineteenth century that many scholars now speak of the Hausa-Fulani as a single ethnic group. This seeming amalgamation resulted from the fact that Fulani became the ruling class over many of the Hausa states during the upheavals of that century. Other pastoral Fulani gave up herding because of drought and cattle diseases in the last century, and became cultivators alongside the Hausa. In both cases, the Fulani tended to lose their original language and become "Hausa-ized." It seems most accurate to think of the hyphenated Fulani among the Hausa in the way that one thinks of Italian-Americans or German-Americans in the United States.

Still, distinct Fulani Populations remain throughout West Africa and even in parts of Nigeria. As a matter of fact, the Fulani of West Africa, according to one authority, "form the largest nomadic society in the world." They and their herds (cattle and sheep) stretch across the Sudan from east of Lake Chad all the way to the Atlantic in Senegal. "Fulani," the term used for these people in English, is from the Hausa word for them; they call themselves the *Fulbe* (plural; singular, *Peul*). The Hausa rulers allowed them to have grazing rights as they moved within or across the territories of Kano, Katsina, Gobir, or Zaria. They were organized under their own clan chiefs, however. There was of course potential conflict between the Hausa farmers and the Fulani herders, because cattle could trample or eat crops and farmers could enclose grazing land. The Hausa rulers also instituted a cattle-tax that appears to have been resented by the Fulani herders. Such resentments of taxes and land enclosures could underlie the animosities brought to the surface in the Fulani jihads of the early 1800s.

The Fulani can be subdivided into the herding, nomadic branch (rural Fulani), and the scholarly, urban branch (known as the *Torodbe*). These latter Fulani became prominent in Islamic affairs, especially in Nigeria among the Hausa. Usually, these Fulani scholars and clerics were members of the *Qadiriyya tariqa*, or brotherhood. It is this last group that led the jihads in the nineteenth century and became the ruling elite of the Hausa; they usually speak Hausa and no longer know the Fulfulde language.

## The Yoruba

The term Yoruba originally referred to the inhabitants of the great empire of Oyo. Eventually, the name came to be applied to all the people of southwestern Nigeria speaking the same language as the people of Oyo. We should note that, as is the case for the Hausa, the Yoruba today represent a more homogeneous group than was probably the case in the past. We have seen that the Yoruba trace their political and religious identity to the city-state of Ife, which was believed to have been the center of the world, the point where the divine being, Oduduwa, first made dry (habitable) land. From Ife the rulers of the various Yoruba states, as well as of Benin, were sent out.

While today Yoruba are scattered throughout communities all over West Africa, about 17 million reside in the southwestern area of Nigeria. Some Yoruba-speakers also live in the neighboring Republic of Benin (formerly Dahomey), as the British and French boundary-makers in colonial times divided the area between them. While the common people known as Yoruba have probably lived in this general vicinity for thousands of years, the legends regarding rulers coming from Ife may indicate a class of invaders from the North (from the Sudan, perhaps) who established their hegemony over the Yoruba.

Traditionally, the Yoruba were town or city dwellers, with smaller farming communities associated with each town or city. The towns were made up of a combination of large family compounds (each compound housing as many as 1,000 people). The compounds were organized around and based upon lineages. These lineages held the farm land in common in areas beyond the boundaries of the town itself. This feature of living in a town some distance from one's farm is distinctive of the Yoruba. Each town at its center had an "*Afin,*" or dwelling place for the town's oba, or chief. The palace normally had a gabled entrance, with an open verandah facing the town's central marketplace. The oba was seen as the townspeople's priest and protector, which could explain the settlement around his residence.

The Yoruba share some distinctive religious beliefs that allow for toleration of newer religions. Today about one-half of the Yoruba of Nigeria are Muslim and many are Christian, but they often feel welcome and comfortable at ceremonies or rituals celebrating the Yoruba traditional beliefs. These traditional beliefs vary from place to place and from time to time; nevertheless, most versions see the universe as consisting of a domain of the sky above and one of the earth beneath, with the habitable world in between.

The domain of the sky is under the dominion of Olorun Oludumare ("Olorun" means "sky-owner"). Olorun is remote from the affairs of people and therefore not prayed to or invoked to meet human needs. The domain of the earth (referring to the earth that supports the cultivable or inhabited part of the visible world) is female, Onilo (earth-owner), but more usually called Ile (the personification of earth); often she is invoked as Iya, "Mother." It is she who receives the souls of the dead.

Beneath Olorun, the ruler of the sky, are the various *orishas*, which may also be referred to as "gods." It is these orishas who involve themselves in affairs of the world. There are principal orishas, who are themselves heads of lineages of lesser orishas—so they are arranged hierarchically. Some of the major orishas include the following: Oduduwa, the founder of Ife and Yoruba culture; Shango, associated with thunder and lightning and the personal orisha of the kings of Oyo; Ogun, the orisha of iron-working (as well as of warriors, barbers, and others whose work depends upon iron); and Oya, the female orisha who is thought of as the wife of Shango and associated with the River Niger. While these orishas, among others, are seen as being part of the sky domain, other orishas are thought of as operating especially in the world of people, for example, Ifa, the orisha of divination; and Eshu, the trickster, associated with market places.

In addition to the orishas, there are also beings of the sky known as *ara-orun* ("sky-people"), who are the spirit doubles of all those people living on the earth or waiting to be born. A sub-set of sky people are the source of "bad" children who die in infancy over and over again, tormenting their mothers. This belief is very likely a folk explanation for the high infant mortality among the people of the tropical regions of West Africa. As we shall see, the Igbo of southeastern Nigeria have a similar explanation for the existence of these "bad" children.

In addition to these beings, the spirits from the earth below, the *Ogboni*, were Ile's (earth's) counterparts to the orishas of Olorun (the sky). Often, the Ogboni seemed to be vengeful spirits, perhaps representing the ancestors among some Yoruba. *Egungun*, the Masks, usually represented sanctions of the ancestors against those who failed to uphold the traditions of the community.

There were cults for each of the major Orishas, for the Ogboni, and for the Egungun. At Oyo, the Ogboni cult was especially important, since it mediated between the council of elders, known as the *Oyo Mesi,* and the ruler, the Alafin. The members of the Ogboni cult were often priests or elders in other cults, so they represented the important leaders throughout Oyo society. The cult of Shango was also especially important in Oyo because Shango was thought of as an Alafin who had been deified. The Alafins made use of the cult of Shango in collecting fees for purification rites throughout Yorubaland and relied upon respect for the cult in extending their power. The Egungun cult was also powerful because the masks were the avenue by which powerful ancestors and some gods were called up to settle the town's business. One of the most powerful of the Egungun was "owned" by the Alafin, which is to say that he kept the mask and assigned the person to wear the mask.

The organization of the universe, as envisioned by the Yoruba, was the basis for the organization of cities and states. Through various offices and cults, society was ordered to reflect the order of the Sky and the Earth.

Politically, the Yoruba were divided into several states of varying size and power, each consisting of several towns, each town with its own oba. As seen above, the state of Oyo was quite large, while among the branch of Yoruba called the Ekiti, states were extremely small. The leading oba in a capital of a state was permitted to wear a beaded crown, hence these capitals were called *ilu alade,* or "crowned towns." The title of the leading oba generally came from the name of the town, as the Olowo of Owo, or the Oni(fe) of Ife, and the Eleko of Eko. The title of Alafin at Oyo, "ruler of the palace," was an exception.

An oba usually led a life of ceremony and ritual, secluded in his afin. He was surrounded by a "cabinet" of leading hereditary chiefs. In Oyo this powerful body was known as the Oyo Mesi (from the Yoruba for "Oyo knows the answers"). The oba was typically chosen from a particular royal male lineage. For example, in Oyo, the Oyo Mesi selected the Alafin from males in the royal family. Some states used divination to determine which member of a lineage would be oba. In certain areas, the obas had to meet certain physical standards. In one small Ekiti state, for example, a candidate could be rejected for being too tall, out of fear that he would look down on his subjects. Women were not necessarily excluded; there are traditions of female obas at Ife, Oyo, Ondo, and Ilesha.

At Oyo, the Alafin did not usually go beyond the verandah of his palace except during the celebration of certain annual rituals. The palace household comprised several kinds of officials and attendants. An important official was the master of the horse, as represented by the character Elesin in Wole Soyinka's play, *Death and the King's Horseman*. He was among several officials expected to commit suicide upon the death of an Alafin in order to accompany the king on his journey into the afterlife. There were high-ranking eunuches who often were stand-ins for the Alafin at various rituals. There was a group of 68 royal slaves, marked by shaved heads, who served as bodyguards and messengers for the king. Another powerful group were the ladies of the court, led by the "*iya oba*," or official mother of the Alafin. (By comparison, the "mother of the market" in Soyinka's play mentioned above is called "*Iyaloja*".) The Alafin's actual mother would have been "invited to go to sleep" and buried when her son became the ruler. In addition were the many royal wives, or queens, and several other female court officials. Three relatives of the Alafin, including his son, titled the *Aremo*, would be designated as official "fathers of the king." The tradition developed in the 1700s that the Aremo, like the King's horseman, would also commit suicide on the death of the Alafin. The eldest son, therefore, could never inherit the throne.

The power of the Yoruba obas, including the Alafin, was restricted in several ways. The government in the Yoruba kingdoms appeared quite confusing to outsiders, no doubt because of the division of responsibilities and authority among so many competing groups. Oyo, because of its prominence, offers the best known example of divided rule. In that empire, the major check on the ruler's power was the *Oyo Mesi*, made up of seven councilors, each of whom held a hereditary title in his own family or lineage. This council had the power to announce the rejection of the Alafin, who on receiving such a message from the council, was obliged to commit suicide. The leader of the council was the *Bashorun*, the main kingmaker and interpreter of the divinations of the Alafin's personal spirit. At the height of Oyo's power, one of these Bashoruns, named

Gaha, became even more powerful than the Alafin, four of whom he had killed. During his "reign" an army of Oyo reportedly even defeated an army of the Ashanti in the West. In 1774, the fifth Alafin to come to power during Gaha's time succeeded in having him killed. This Alafin, Abiodun, reigned over a time of peace and prosperity, a calm before the storm of the decline of Oyo and the violent upheavals among the Yoruba of the nineteenth century. The famous Oyo cavalry was never as effective after the death of Abiodun in 1789.

Patrilineal descent groups, or lineages as described in the first section of this chapter, were the basic social organization of the Yoruba people. Because the lineages were patrilineal, women could not become heads of these groups, but in many Yoruba cities the women were represented in governmental councils by a woman chief, usually titled the *Iyalode*. Again, Soyinka's *Death and the King's Horseman* offers a singular example of a powerful woman, Iyaloja, playing a prominent role in a Yoruba society. Throughout much of West Africa, the local marketplaces were preeminently the sphere of the market women, who would be led by a woman such as Iyaloja.

The major occupation of the people was farming, even though most were town dwellers. Many farmers also practiced various crafts such as weaving and working in iron, or involved themselves in long-distance trade during seasons not conducive to farming.

Yoruba society included several categories of persons not considered free. In addition to slavery, there was a condition known as *iwofa*, a temporary pawning of a person or his or her child to pay off a debt or to raise money. As among the Hausa, royal slaves could become powerful civil or military servants. There were classes of slaves for working farms and serving in households as well. Also, as among the Hausa, slaves were acquired mainly as war captives, but criminals and debtors could also fall into this condition. Because warfare with other peoples produced so many of the slaves, many were non-Yoruba, which could be a destabilizing influence. Hausa slaves in Oyo's province of Ilorin seem to have provided the forces for an uprising against Oyo there during the time of the Fulani jihads, as described later.

## The Igbo

As noted in regard to the ethnic identifications of the Hausa and Yoruba, the Igbo probably had no overarching notion of an Igbo ethnic identity before very recent times. Even today, some Igbo-speaking groups, especially those living west of the Niger River, reject the designation of Igbo. The word "Igbo," originally meaning "community of people" or "the people," acquired connotations suggesting "forest dwellers," "bush men," or "backwardness." Such connotations could have easily led to the rejection of the term among these people and other Igbo-speakers. The term only began to be accepted in the 1940s when a kind of national consciousness developed among the Igbo as they realized they had political and economic interests in common.[6]

The Igbo lived in small farming villages scattered throughout the densely forested region of southeastern Nigeria. For the most part, Igbo polities consisted of very small-scale societies. Kingship was rare among them, although not unknown. In the western part of Igboland, near the sphere of Benin, there was the Kingdom of Onitsha, with an Obi, or king (note the similarity with Oba). The position of Obi was not hereditary, however; he was elected from among the residents of certain villages. These elections are hotly contested even in the present day.

The typical Igbo polities were organized at two levels: the village and the village-group. Each village was essentially sovereign and ruled through direct participatory democracy. Three to six (occasionally more) villages in a small geographical area could also be associated in a village-group. The issues that the village group could take up were restricted by various kinds of traditional charters, or founding myths. In deliberations at this level, each village had equal representation and was required to make equal contributions to undertakings of the village-group. Important decisions usually required unanimity of all the villages. When they conquered this area, the British as well as other outsiders, were surprised to find so dense a population maintaining apparent order and stability without centralized political structures.

Villages comprised several compounds, each with a compound head who had some authority in areas of work assignments, ritual, and so on. Each compound consisted of several households which formed the extended family. Some compound heads were also lineage heads, and so had ritual functions that went with leadership of the lineage. Among the Igbo, the lineages were usually patrilineal.

The village rather than a centralized state, therefore, was the focus of politics, law, and order. Leadership positions within the village normally were held by titled men and women. Legislative functions were exercised by councils consisting of all adult males of the village. Everyone present could speak on any issue being debated, but following the discussion, the lineage heads would retire from the meeting room for a consultation. When the consultation was finished, the best orator among the heads would be selected to give the decision to the rest of the assembly. Issues dealt with could include regulating markets, setting prices, firing bush for farming purposes, or deciding on peace and war.

Legal cases often were handled by the same assembly of adult males. The assembly lacked any coercive function in enforcing its decisions, however. A man found guilty of murder, for example, was expected to hang himself—there was no community right to inflict capital punishment. The villagers could bring social pressure on the criminal, but that was all. If the culprit fled, his kinship group was expected to flee also and give up all its property. The operation of these sanctions are illustrated in Achebe's novel, *Things Fall Apart*, in the actions of the main protagonist, Okonkwo. After accidentally shooting a relative, Okonkwo and his extended family immediately flee to his mother's home village. His good friends, after helping the family on their way, destroy Okonkwo's compound and all his property. No one tells him or his friends to take these actions: they all understand their obligations implicitly.

The Igbo world view envisioned interaction between the world of the living and the world of the "dead," or of the spirits. The second world included the ancestors as well as those who had not yet been born. The Igbo high god was, like Olorun of the Yoruba, withdrawn from the world, his creative work completed. There were various titles for the high god, depending upon the characteristic being emphasized. Often, this god was referred to as Chukwu (the Great God).

Below Chukwu were various nature gods. One of the most important of these was Ala or Ani, the earth goddess, who is closest to people of this world (compare Ile of the Yoruba). She was the great mother who must be appeased in any matter relating to land or the earth (such as the sale of property). Usually benevolent, Ala was responsible for punishing major offenses, such as incest; one found to be guilty of such an offense was denied burial in the ground. There was also a sun god who helped crops and trees to grow.

Large rivers, such as the Niger, were felt to have spiritual force as well. In addition there were spirits of forests and other places, spirit doubles for individuals, and the "bad" children (called *ogbanje*) who die in infancy or early childhood only to be reborn and die again. This belief is illustrated in Achebe's *Things Fall Apart*. The favorite daughter of Okonkwo, the main character, is thought to be an ogbanje. A spiritual healer, however, succeeded in having Ezinma, the daughter, lead him to the secret, buried charm that connected her to the spirit world of the ogbanje, and thereby ended the cycle. As noted earlier such a belief, also found among the Yoruba, probably represents an attempt to explain the high rate of infant mortality along the West African coast where malaria is endemic.

Comparable to the Egungun cults among the Yoruba were *Egwugwu* cults. The Egwugwu appeared among the Igbo often to help resolve disputes or to deal with those accused of wrongdoing. This practice is again well-described by Achebe in his novel of traditional Igbo life. In one chapter, the Egwugwu come forth from their special hut, instilling awe and fright among the women and children of the village. Arranging themselves on stools in order of seniority, entirely covered in raffia, with carved and painted masks where faces should be, the "dead fathers of the clan" hear and settle disputes among the villagers.

Many functions in life were accompanied by rituals and sacrifices. Three major rituals were associated with the stages of the yam-growing cycle, for example, including a major thanksgiving festival associated with the yam harvest. Nearly all Igbo were farmers, cultivating several types of yam and harvesting oil from the oil palm trees of the region. It is not surprising, therefore, that rituals and ceremonies were closely related to their farming activities. *Things Fall Apart* again provides a description of the importance of the New Yam Festival, which was in many ways a new year celebration, initiating a season of plenty and new beginnings. Feasting, dancing and drumming, and highly popular wrestling matches were enjoyed during the festival.

There were also specialists associated with the spiritual well-being of the Igbo communities. Special persons associated with divination and ritual were called *dibia*, a term loosely applied to various kinds of seers, diviners, and magicians. Rainmakers were also important specialists, passing on their special skill from father to son through the generations.

Oracles were also traditionally important among the Igbo, serving to establish links among Igbo communities over wide geographical areas. The oracle in a particular region had a judicial function in serving as a court of appeals or of last resort in criminal cases, offenses against the gods, or disputes among individuals. The most famous of these oracles was the *ibini okpabe* of the Aro Chukwu Igbo. The Aro were originally a village group of about nine villages (later nineteen) which had traders throughout Igboland. The Aro also served as agents of their oracle, investigating cases that were referred to it.

Most Igbo in the villages were considered to be freeborn, full citizens (known as *diala*) of the community. Persons of less than full citizen status were called *ohu*; these included slaves and "pawns" (individuals who were indentured for a specified period of time for debt payment or other obligation but who were not considered slaves). The *ohu* could eventually be absorbed into the lineage of the compound to which they were attached and their origins forgotten. Such was not the case with the very specialized group known as osu, descendants of persons who had been dedicated for service to a deity. *Osu* could never be absorbed into normal kinship patterns. In Chinua Achebe's novel, *No Longer at Ease*, a sequel to *Things Fall Apart*, Okonkwo's grandson Obi falls in love with a woman who, he later learns, is *osu*. Even Obi's family, now converted to Christianity, reject the possibility that he could even consider marriage to such a person.

Although we think of the Igbo as living in independent, small-scale societies, links connected Igbo to one another. Titled societies with special initiation fees and ceremonies provided for pan-Igbo associations. Membership in such societies conferred coveted status on the title-takers. The oracles and their agents provided another kind of linkage, as did associations of diviners, the *dibia* societies, found throughout the homeland of the Igbo.

Until colonial times, there was almost no history of warfare except small-scale affairs pitting one village or village-group against another. The tiny states had no standing armies, of course. Every man stood ready to arm himself and go out and fight a battle for his village as the need arose and then return to his farming. Occasionally, groups of hot-headed or restless young men would feature themselves as "warriors" or even "headhunters," but they were not widely accepted. In the border areas of Igboland, however, martial traditions were usually stronger. In the southern border region, the Aro village-group, or clan, began to use the power of their famous oracle to collect slaves from among the other Igbo villages. The Aro took advantage of warrior classes of so-called "headhunters" that had developed most notably among the village-groups of Abam and Ohafia to serve as their military guards and mercenaries in the furtherance of Aro slave-trading activities. The particularly fierce reputations of the Abam and Ohafia are remembered still today.

The Igbo are a huge, ancient group of people located mainly in Southeastern Nigeria. Despite their dense population they did not, for the most part, develop large, centralized states; each village or small village-group was sovereign and independent. Their experience thus contrasts with that of the very closely-related Edo people who formed the powerful kingdom of Benin just to the west of the Igbo. For the most part, the Igbo in their heartland remained somewhat isolated from the effects of international trade and political upheavals until fairly recent times. On the fringes of this heartland, however, among the Igbo living west of the Niger or the peoples like the Aro or Ohafia, these external forces had more impact. The Aro, with their Ohafia and Abam allies, became very much involved in the Atlantic slave trade.

## Summary

This brief summary of these three traditional societies of Nigeria reveals that they have not been static or unchanging. Many of the traditions of the Hausa have been integrated into the larger tradition of Islam. The Yoruba and Igbo also exhibit complex world views worked out over a long period of time dealing with internal changes as well as external forces represented by trade and aggressive neighbors. These people all were predominantly dependent upon agriculture—grain in the north and root crops, especially the yam, in the south. International forces and trade had more impact on the northern, Hausa peoples at first, but the reorientation of the trade, resulting from the extension of the Sudanic system toward the south and the appearance of European traders at the Coast, were to have important repercussions for the Igbo and Yoruba, as well. The rate of change accelerated with the coming of Europeans to the West African coastal region. In following sections we will see that the Atlantic slave trade, the ending of the slave trade, and the European imposition of colonial rule over Nigeria resulted in changes more violent and sudden than those of the prior centuries.

## Notes

1 Victor Uchendu, *The Igbo of Southeast Nigeria*, New York: Holt, Rinehart, and Winston, 1965, p. 12.

2 Luigi M. Solivetti, "Family, Marriage and Divorce in a Hausa Community: A Sociological Model," *Africa* 64 (1994), 252–253.

3 Solivetti, 256.

4 Richard E. Weekes, *Muslim Peoples: A World Ethnographic Survey*, 2nd ed. Westport, CT: Greenwood Press, 1984, p. 257.

5 Robert S. Smith, *Kingdoms of the Yoruba*, 3rd. ed. Madison, WI: University of Wisconsin Press, 1988, p. 93.

6 Don C. Ohandike, *Anioma: A Social History of the Western Igbo People*, Athens, OH: Ohio University Press, 1994, pp. 27–28.

# THE COMING OF COLONIAL NIGERIA: THE 19TH CENTURY

People throughout the African continent began to experience significant changes in their lives in the nineteenth century as a result of increasing contact with Europeans, who had until this century mainly confined their activities to the coast. By the end of the century, European states had carved up nearly the entire continent among themselves, initiating the colonial period in Africa. Even before European power reached into the interior, many parts of Africa suffered various destabilizing wars and internal migrations.

In West Africa the main precursors of these kinds of change were the effects of the Atlantic slave trade and its suppression by the British and the internal political changes wrought by a series of Islamic holy wars, or jihads, in the savanna country of the interior. This chapter discusses these two phenomena in turn. We begin first with some historical background concerning the Atlantic slave trade before turning to the effects of its abolition in the 1800s.

## European Trade at the Coast—Development of the Slave Trade

The Portuguese began working their way gradually down the west coast of Africa under the energetic guidance of Prince Henry the Navigator. Beginning in 1415 Prince Henry sent out expedition after expedition, hoping to find a route around Africa to the rich trade of the East.

In 1481 the Portuguese founded a major post on the Gold Coast (modern Ghana), *Sao Jorge de Mina* (Elmina Castle), to trade for the gold from the interior. By 1482 they had made contact with Benin and had reached the mouth of the Congo River. Bartolomeo Dias rounded the Cape of Good Hope (then called by the Europeans the Cape of

Storms) and sailed into the Indian Ocean in 1487–88. Later expeditions, beginning with that of Vasco da Gama, took them on into the world of the Indian Ocean where they established a maritime empire stretching from Goa in India, to Malacca in the East Indies, and to Mombasa in East Africa.

Along the West African coast the Portuguese set up permanent establishments. Ambassadors were exchanged with Benin, and efforts were made to Christianize the vast empire of the Mani-Kongo inland from the mouth of the Congo River. South of the Congo area the Portuguese attempted to establish a feudal state and encouraged Portuguese settlers in the lands of rulers known as the Ngola; Angola remained a Portuguese colony for 400 years.

Early on, the Portuguese discovered the value of trading in African slaves taken from the West African coast. Minor on-shore slave raids took place as early as 1441 and 1443. Trade soon replaced raids as the standard method for obtaining the slaves. For example, the Portuguese became involved in trading horses and firearms to feuding branches of the Wolof (in modern Senegal) in return for war captives as early as 1448. The Island of Sao Tome, just south of Nigeria in the Atlantic, became an important sugar producing colony for the Portuguese who began to import large numbers of slaves from Benin and the domain of the Mani-Kongo.

Soon the larger sea powers of Europe, such as England and France, became involved. At first, these newcomers sought mainly items such as gold (an English coin became known as a Guinea, from the name of the region from which the gold came in West Africa), ivory, pepper, and palm oil. The discoveries in the New World, however, began to increase the demand for cheap labor, first for the mines of Central and South America and then for the sugar-plantations on the Caribbean islands. The Spanish crown took over the licensing of shipments of slaves to the Spanish colonies in the Americas, and this became a major source of revenue for the Spanish government. Eventually the English obtained this franchise and became the largest carrier of African slaves to the Americas. The Dutch succeeded in taking over many of the richest parts of the far-flung Portuguese empire in the 1600s (taking Elmina in 1638, for example). The English, French, Dutch, and Danes all acquired sugar producing West Indian colonies also in the 1600s, leading to a further increase in the demand for slave labor. Thus, European economic exploitation of Africa inaugurated a process of change in traditional Africa, the effects of which are felt even today. It is the traditional organization of African societies and the changes brought about by European intervention to which we now turn our attention.

In descriptions of Hausa, Yoruba, and Igbo cultures, we have noted the existence of various categories of people, some of which included a traditional servile or slave status. These traditional states of slavery were normally quite different from the chattel slavery that became the basis of the long-distance slave trade of the Europeans or Arabs. A wide range of human relationships was possible in traditional Africa. In many cases, these relationships amounted to what can be termed "rights-in-persons," meaning that some people had rights over the labor and lives of others. In a simple case, a husband could expect wives to provide labor for the family farm, and fathers had similar rights over the labor of children. In other cases, individuals could hire themselves or dependents out to secure or pay off a debt. "Strangers" (those outside the local kinship system) often found themselves in similar dependent situations. Prisoners acquired in wars or sent as tribute could fall into such dependency. A group (village, lineage, family compound) or an individual might have the right of disposing of "strangers" by selling or trading them to others.

Under what circumstances could these "acquired strangers" be defined as "slaves" in the usual Western sense? This question is difficult to answer. Some dependent people eventually could become integrated into the kinship group of the "masters," losing their slave status. Once emancipated, they might acquire property, including other people who could be considered slaves. Status in society could vary, as well. Some "acquired strangers," or slaves, filled important roles in government and administration. Others—the *Osu* slaves of Igbo tradition, for example—could never change their status. European interest in slaves from the African coast created a sudden, huge demand for people who, in one way or another, had fallen into one of these "slave" categories. As the demand grew, so did practices such as slave-raiding and warfare to acquire prisoners, a process which destabilized African "dependency" traditions and, as we shall see, in many cases the social and economic fabric of West African society.

The demographic effects of the slave trade on Africa are difficult to assess accurately. Many slave-traders kept poor records, and we can make only rough estimates about how many slaves were transported across the Atlantic or the Sahara. There is no way of knowing how many people were killed in raids and wars to acquire slaves, nor the extent of crop destruction and subsequent famine. Scholars estimate that nearly twelve million people were transported as slaves from Africa toward the Americas between 1450 and 1900. About 50% of these people were sent from Africa during the 1700s and nearly 30% during the nineteenth century.[1] The greatest period of demand coincided with the greatest expansion of the sugarcane industry from Brazil north through the Caribbean. The social and political effects of the slave trade were of great significance, and we now turn to those issues.

## Impact of the Slave Trade

These effects were no doubt experienced unevenly by different African societies. Losses to specific groups varied according to location, political organization, and other factors. A marked preference for young, adult males meant that potential farmers, fathers, and warriors were lost in large numbers by some peoples. The abduction of so many men of similar age brought about tremendous imbalance and disruption in African communities which were organized along traditional gender divisions.

Throughout Africa, states arose that depended directly or indirectly on the slave trade. Although it may oversimplify some of the complexities of specific cases, one can think of an exchange of firearms for human beings as the engine driving the system. Centralized states near the coast found that they were in a position to acquire guns with which to demand tribute (payable in slaves) or to make war on neighbors. To protect themselves, some of the neighbors found it expedient to get involved in this trade in order to get the military hardware necessary for their own defense. Thus, the European demand for slave labor at once exacerbated internecine warfare and increased its destructive capability.

In the Niger Delta, the "People of the Salt Water" (mainly Ijo, Ibibio, and related peoples) controlled access to the inland water routes. Important cities controlling outlets to the Niger and Cross Rivers became dependent on the wealth of the slave trade: these towns included Bonny (Ibani), New Calabar and Old Calabar (Kalabari), Cross Town, Duke Town, and others. The trading houses of the cities served as intermediaries, collecting slaves from the interior (from among the Igbo, usually) and trading them to British, Dutch, and other European slavers stationed in ships anchored off the coast. These towns fell under the rule of the trading houses which became, in effect, merchant oligarchies. These houses dealt through the important Igbo oracle of the Aro-Chukwu (known to Europeans as the "Long Juju"), as described in the previous chapter. Because the Aro-Chukwu oracle served as a court of last resort for the Igbo and because captured slaves were used as a kind of human currency, the oracle's fines were frequently "paid" in slaves, who were then sold to one of the coastal trading houses. In the last chapter, we saw that as the Aro slave trade became more highly organized, they resorted more frequently to the use of warrior groups from the Igbo villages of Ohafia, Abam, and others. These Ohafia or Abam warriors became the soldiers and guards for the Aro slave-trading expeditions.

West of the Niger Delta, the Empire of Benin was an early source of slaves for the Portuguese sugar plantations on Sao Tome, but after dynastic wars ended and the expansion of the empire slowed in the seventeenth century, its role in that trade declined. Pepper, ivory, and cloth were still traded to the Europeans, however. Following 1700, new wars involving Benin led to the sale of war captives in return for the importation of firearms. Benin became increasingly dependent on this guns-for-slaves trade on into the nineteenth century, leading to a decline in the prosperity and power of the state.

North and west of Benin, the Yoruba empire of Oyo grew in the 1700s as a result of slave labor on royal farms. These slaves were acquired by warfare and from trade with the north (the Sudanic trading network). The wars "produced" more captives than were needed for Oyo's internal use, though, and many were sent to the coast for sale to the Europeans in return for firearms, cloth, and cowrie shells (used as currency). The royal establishment became overdependent on this trade, and after 1780, when the demand for slaves at the coast declined during the Napoleonic Wars, this state also went into decline. This period coincides with the end of the reign of the Alafin Abiodun, as described in the previous chapter.

Strife between the Alafins, the kings of Oyo, and the increasingly powerful head of the council of elders, or Oyo, Mesi, weakened the state in the closing stages of the eighteenth century, as we have seen. Wars broke out among the other Yoruba states and Oyo. Dahomey, formerly a dependency of Oyo and much involved in the slave trade after the 1720s, warred incessantly with Oyo and other neighbors in an effort to expand its power as an independent empire. All these events served to further undermine the power and stability of Oyo.

In northern Nigeria, the Hausa states looked toward the north and the trans-Saharan trade rather than toward the south and the Atlantic slave trade. Zaria, in the southern part of Hausaland, was the city-state traditionally most involved in the slave trade. This state provided the other Hausa states with many of the slaves they used for internal farming and for shipment across the Sahara to Arabic countries of North Africa. Kanem-Bornu, far from the gold sources that had fueled the trading empires of the Sudanic Kingdoms to the west, was always more dependent on the trans-Saharan slave trade than the other Sudanic empires.

By roughly the year 1800, a vast and long-standing trading network based largely on slaves in many locations had developed along the coast of West Africa, affecting states and people far into the interior. This established economy and working relationship between and among Africans and Europeans were about to be upset in the new century by a concerted effort to abolish the hated slave trade and replace it with a new economic base and a new relationship, eventually a colonial relationship, between Africans and Europeans.

## The Ending of the Slave Trade

The huge expansion of the sugar industry, which correlated with the largest volume of the Atlantic slave trade, led to over-production and falling prices by the end of the eighteenth century. In England especially, investment in new manufacturing enterprises which were not dependent on imported slave labor began to appear more attractive. In these circumstances, humanitarian movements for the abolition of the slave trade and eventually of slavery could receive a hearing in an England embarking on the "Industrial Revolution." An organized British anti-slavery campaign began around 1765 initiated by Evangelicals and Quakers and led by people such as Granville Sharp, Thomas Claxton, and William Wilberforce. Rescued former African slaves like the famous Olaudah Equiano, himself an Igbo, also took part in publicizing this campaign.

Abolition, however, was a long, drawn-out process. First slavery was outlawed in England itself; then the trade in slaves was ended;

finally, slavery was abolished throughout the British Empire and in other nations. The first stage was successfully concluded as early as 1772 with the Mansfield Decision. British abolitionists had rescued a slave from an American who had taken the slave to England. When the American regained his "property," the abolitionists brought a writ of *habeas corpus* to secure the slave's release. The Chief Justice, Lord Mansfield, held that slavery was in itself odious, or hateful, on its face and therefore needed a law specifically legalizing it rather than a law making it specifically illegal. Since there was no such law, all slaves who touched English soil (in England itself; not elsewhere in the British Empire) were immediately and automatically freed.

Both the Mansfield Decision and the American Revolutionary War, which resulted in many slaves fleeing from the new United States into Canada, led to a growing population of freed African slaves in London and Canada. Granville Sharp reportedly first came up with the idea of "repatriation," sending the freed slaves to a settlement in West Africa. In 1787 an expedition with 400 or 450 freed slaves was sent from London to the area of Sierra Leone in West Africa, where the abolitionists hoped to acquire land for a settlement. Many of these freed slaves were several generations removed from their ancestors' deportation from Africa and very few, of course, would have come from the Sierra Leone area. After difficulties with the local people, which led to the near-extinction of the colony, a large immigration of 1792 from Nova Scotia and in 1800 from Jamaica led to a firmer foundation at the settlement called Freetown.

A joint stock company was organized to help finance the new settlement. The Church Missionary Society (CMS), founded by Wilberforce in 1799, was also an important force in supporting this experiment in repatriation. In 1808, Sierra Leone became a Crown Colony, which meant that the British government took responsibility for protecting and maintaining the settlement. This colony was to have an important effect along the West African coast and was to become important in the later history of Nigeria. In his *History of the African People,* Robert July explains: "Although very few of the inhabitants native to Sierra Leone were affected, the rise in the Freetown area of a Christian community of African repatriates, learning English and gradually becoming Europeanized, was a development of great consequence and a cast a long shadow."[2] A large proportion of freed slaves brought to Freetown in the nineteenth century were Yoruba, because the Yoruba civil wars following the breakup of the Oyo empire provided large numbers of war captives for the trade.

The other famous experiment in the repatriation of freed slaves was in Liberia where Americans established another settlement of freed slaves at Monrovia (established during the presidency of James Monroe, 1822). The U.S. was always ambiguous about its relationship with Liberia and never officially claimed Liberia as a colony. The first black governor, J. J. Roberts, was not installed until 1841. After the European powers insisted on knowing the status of this settlement, it formally declared its independence in 1847. The United States, however, did not recognize that independence until 1862. The French also established a small, freed slave settlement at the town of Libreville in the area that became the French colony of Gabon.

Meanwhile, the campaign against the slave trade continued, with Great Britain in the forefront. In 1807, an act of Parliament made it illegal for British subjects to engage in the trade. The following year, 1808, was the year the United States had set for its own abolition of the trade (not slavery itself) as a result of the compromises at the Constitutional Convention of 1787. The tiny country of Denmark outlawed its own trade in 1803. Other European countries followed suit over the next several years. Still, the British were the most stringent in enforcing the anti-slave trade laws. They established a permanent naval patrol in West African waters to enforce the ban. As a result of reciprocal treaties with several other nations, the patrol gained the authority to stop and search the ships of several nations in ail effort to suppress the trade. The effectiveness of this anti-slavery effort is not clear. Well over a million slaves appear to have been landed in the Americas between 1825 and 1865, when the end of the American Civil War had the effect of reducing demand significantly.

The British abolitionists hoped to supplement the naval policy of interdiction with a policy of providing economic alternatives for African societies dependent on the slave trade. This policy was based on spreading Christianity, commerce, and colonization. Both the policy of suppression and the policy for ending African dependence on slavery meant increasing British involvement in local affairs along the West African coast, especially in areas such as Lagos where Yoruba slaves were being shipped, and the Niger Delta where the trading houses were collecting Igbo captives.

The Creoles (as the repatriates were called) from Sierra Leone joined in this struggle against the slave trade. A college was established, the famous Fourah Bay College, in Sierra Leone In 1827 to train Africans to participate in missionary efforts along the coast. The first student was Samuel Ajayi Crowther, a Yoruba youth who had been repatriated to Freetown in 1822. He went on to seminary in England and was later posted to a CMS mission in Abeokuta among the Yoruba in 1845. In 1864, Crowther became the bishop in charge of administering several CMS mission stations in Nigeria. In this role, Crowther began to formulate ideas for African independent states on a European model.

A second generation Sierra Leonian, James Africanus Beale Horton, further systematized such thinking regarding modern African nationalism. Born in 1835 of Igbo parents, he was educated at Fourah Bay College and in Edinburgh, Scotland, where he received his M.D. He became a medical officer in the British Army, returned to West Africa in 1859, and wrote extensively on tropical medicine and African politics. Horton maintained two basic principles in his political writings: that there was no physical or intellectual difference between Africans and Europeans, and that the process of social improvement he observed among the Africans would have to end in the establishment of new free nations in West Africa.

By the middle of the nineteenth century cities were developing along the coast with an orientation that could be described as Western or European—St. Louis in Senegal, a French colony; Monrovia in Liberia; Cape Coast and Accra on the Gold Coast (modern Ghana); Lagos in Nigeria; and, of course, Freetown, home by 1850 to probably 40,000 freed slaves or their descendants. Such westernization did not develop from a conscious policy in London or Paris, but from the effects of growing commercial and political involvement as the British especially tried to develop new legitimate forms of commerce with West Africans to replace slave trading.

The case of the Niger Delta region is a good example of how this European involvement at the coast developed. The area was known to the British and other Europeans as the Oil Rivers ("Oil" referring to palm kernel oil and "Rivers" because it had not been clear to the Europeans that the many creeks and inlets of that area constituted the delta of a single great river). Palm kernel oil had become important as a lubricant because petroleum was not yet widely available for this purpose. The British appointed a consul for the Oil Rivers area in 1849, who became involved in disputes with the various delta cities over the slave trade. In 1854, the use of quinine to avoid malaria came into use, allowing European traders in steam ships to begin penetrating up the Niger River, bypassing the trading houses of coastal towns such as Bonny and Calabar.

In 1879, the very successful trading company of Sir George Goldie Taubman was inaugurated and quickly established a near monopoly on trade on the lower Niger. This company began to fulfill quasi-governmental roles along the river, especially after its designation as a company with a royal charter. Still, no official protectorate was extended over the Oil Rivers by the British until 1885, when other European powers, especially Germany and France, suddenly began to proclaim official protectorates over areas of Africa in the vicinity of Nigeria. In these circumstances, to forestall French and German ambitions in the region, Goldie's company gained its charter as the Royal Niger Company.

The resistance of some of the more centralized states against the growing European presence at the coast of West Africa also led to direct British and French control of parts of the coast. For example, in 1872 the Dutch turned over to the British the fort at Elmina Castle, an action which led to British conflict with the Ashanti Empire (which claimed ownership over the coastal area). The ensuing British-Ashanti War of 1873–74 resulted in a British protectorate over the coastal area in 1874. Ironically, this protectorate forestalled the efforts of Africanus Horton to develop a constitution for an independent Fanti state in the same area. The French found themselves in a similar conflict with the empire of Dahomey beginning in the 1870s which eventually led to the boundary between British and French spheres of influence, cutting across Yorubaland, as was noted earlier.

In Nigeria a similar process resulted in a British colony at Lagos in southwestern Nigeria. In 1851, the British consul from the Oil Rivers, with British military support, replaced one reigning king of Lagos (the Eleko) with another. The British hoped that the new king would be more cooperative in helping to prevent slave trading. The British at Lagos then found themselves embroiled in internal wars among the Yoruba in the hinterland, leading to the establishment of an official British colony at Lagos in 1861. Continued strife with the Egba branch of the Yoruba ultimately resulted in the expulsion of the

CMS mission station at Abeokuta, the one originally set up by Crowther.

The ending of the slave trade and the extension of new commercial ventures by the British in the Nigerian area resulted in the gradual extension of British official. involvement all along the coast of Nigeria. This involvement rapidly accelerated during the period of the so-called "Scramble for Africa" by the Europeans in the last fifteen years of the century. The "Scramble," which initiates the colonial period, is further described in the following chapter. We now turn our attention to the second of the major events that began the reorganization of political life in the interior regions of Nigeria.

## The Fulani Jihad

While the people of southern Nigeria were experiencing the profound changes associated with the ending of the slave trade, the Hausa in the north experienced a revolutionary upheaval and reorganization of their own. A powerful centralized state united the Hausa kingdoms in a new Islamic empire under the rule of the Fulani. Recall that the pastoral Fulani are found throughout the West African Sudan. Two branches had developed: the nomadic herding peoples of the rural countryside and the Islamicized town Fulani.

These town Fulani were often called the *Torodbe*. Sometimes thought of as a Fulani clan, the Torodbe are more accurately conceived of as a society of *ulama* (Islamic scholars) drawn from several ethnic groups—Wolof, Hausa, and Mandinke as well as Fulani. The Torodbe nevertheless came to be identified with the Fulani; they spoke Fulfulde, the Fulani language, married Fulani women, and traveled about with the Fulani. The Torodbe provided the leadership for a series of Islamic uprisings resulting in the establishment of Islamic states throughout West Africa. Beginning in the western part of the Sudanic corridor in the 1700s, Torodbe imams became rulers of small Islamic theocratic states. They came to power by overthrowing traditional leaders who did not seem, to the Torodbe, to be strict enough in their observances of Islamic law and practice. These jihads became part of the tradition of the Torodbe, influencing important jihadists of the nineteenth century, of whom the most famous of all was Uthman dan Fodio (or, Usumanu dan Fodio) in northern Nigeria. The jihad that shook Nigeria, therefore, should be seen as part of a movement widespread in West Africa.

The leaders of these major jihads were members of important Sudanic *tariqas* (sufi orders or brotherhoods). Uthman dan Fodio was a member of the Qadiriyya brotherhood founded by Abd al-Qadir in the twelfth century. The followers of these brotherhoods believed that the thirteenth century after the *hegira* (the date in 622 when the Prophet Muhammed emigrated from Mecca to Medina) would be a millennial age. Many Muslims in West Africa expected a leader to arise as the twelfth in a line of great jihad leaders to renew the struggle for the purification of Islam. Some believed that Askia Muhammed of Songhai had been the eleventh of these anticipated reformers. Uthman dan Fodio, as well as other great jihad leaders in West Africa of the nineteenth century, claimed to be on a mission to restore the purity of Islamic society among the faithful in West Africa. Uthman dan Fodio testified to a mystical vision he had experienced in 1794 in which Muhammed the Prophet and Abd al-Qadir, the founder of the Qadiriyya, commissioned him to "unsheath the Sword of Truth" against the enemies of Islam in West Africa.

Throughout the Islamicized area of West Africa, the Sudanic savannas in which the great trading empires had risen and fallen, there had long been tension between the orthodox Muslim leaders and the traditional rulers, who professed Islam but permitted traditional practices to continue in order to maintain their legitimacy with the people. At an earlier time, we observed how this tension led to instability in the Mali and Songhai states, as in the overthrow of Sunni Ali's dynasty of Songhai by Askia Muhammed the Great. The early eighteenth century jihads in the far Western region of the Sudanic corridor similarly resulted from this tension between the devout and those seen as pragmatic compromisers. By the end of the eighteenth century the Hausa states, in which the rulers had grown corrupt and remote from the common people, were ripe for Islamic revolution.

Uthman dan Fodio, born in 1754 in the northern Hausa state of Gobir, began teaching around age 20. The *Fodiawa*, as his family was known in Hausa, were already distinguished scholars and teachers in the tradition of Sunni Islam and inclined toward Muslim reform. The ruler, or Sarki, of Gobir became suspicious of dan Fodio's preaching against misgovernment, and there may have been an attempt on Uthman dan Fodio's life around 1789. During the 1790s his preaching seemed to grow more militant, leading to an edict by the ruler that none of his followers would be allowed to teach or preach in Gobir (dan Fodio himself seems to have been too powerful to suffer this restriction). The veneration that people had for Uthman dan Fodio is revealed in a series of miracle stories told about him. For example, a Hausa *maduga* (leader of a caravan) capsized in his canoe full of kola nuts while crossing the Niger. The *maduga* called upon the great Shehu (title of Uthman dan Fodio) to save him, promising a gift of ten calabashes (large gourds used as baskets) full of kolas. At that exact point in time, the Shehu was preaching in Sokoto; he paused, however, to wring water out of the sleeve of his garment and continued preaching. At the same time, the *maduga* felt a powerful hand lift his boat from raging waters to safety. Upon arriving at Sokoto several days later, the trader found Uthman dan Fodio and offered him three calabashes of kolas in gratitude for his rescue. The Shehu gently reminded him, however, that he had promised ten calabashes.[3] The story not only reveals a belief in Uthman dan Fodio's power, but also reminds one of the importance of the kola trade to the Hausa.

A new Sarki, said to have been a student of dan Fodio's, openly attacked him upon coming to power in 1802. Uthman dan Fodio proclaimed jihad in 1804 against the Hausa rulers, turning military command over to his son, Muhammed Bello (or Muhammedu Bello in Hausa form). By 1808, the capital of Gobir, the city of Alkalawa, had fallen to the Fulani jihadists. The Fulani flocked to his banner and by 1811 all of Hausaland was under control of forces loyal to the great Shehu. The jihad in areas outside Gobir, in Kano, Zaria, or Borno for instance, were carried on by Fulani clan leaders, recognized as "flag-bearers" for Uthman dan Fodio. These leaders, when successful, became his Emirs, or deputies, in newly established territories. After Uthman dan Fodio retired from active service in 1812, Uthman's son Muhammed Bello became the Sultan of the empire based on the new center of Sokoto. The rulers of the Hausa states were replaced by the emirs, as we have seen, who were subordinate to the Sultan of Sokoto.

The Fulani forces also pushed on beyond the Hausa states, attacking the Jukun state in the region of the Benue, moving toward the state of Kanem-Borno to the north and east, and toward the Yoruba state of Oyo to the south. New emirates continued to be carved out of these and other areas.

Thousands of Hausa and Fulani slaves throughout the realms of the Yoruba revolted and fled to the northern Yoruba city of Ilorin where civil strife between the traditional ruler of Oyo, the Alafin, and Muslim-led rebels ultimately led to a Muslim victory. The son of a Muslim mallam became the new ruler, or emir, and gave his allegiance to the Empire of Sokoto in the North. Ilorin thus broke away from the Empire of Oyo, beginning the disintegration of the largest Yoruba state and a period of great instability and warfare among the Yoruba.

Kanem-Borno, now usually referred to simply as Borno, had lost much of its earlier strength. Still, some of the Hausa states such as Kano and Katsina owed tribute to the Mais; for that reason, the Sarkis of Kano and Daura called on the Mai of Borno for assistance against the jihad launched by Uthman dan Fodio. Such assistance was defeated easily as Kano fell to the Fulani, encouraging some of the Fulani to carry the attack into Borno itself. Some small emirates were established in areas formerly part of Borno and even the capital was captured in 1808. The Mai turned for help to another remarkable Islamic leader, a Muslim scholar and leader of the pastoral Kanembu people, al-Kanemi. This new leader took on Muhammed Bello's forces in argument as well as in battle, and managed to retake most of the Borno state. Although al-Kanemi was the real power in the state, he did leave the Mai on the throne. He instituted changes making Borno a Muslim theocracy.

Meanwhile, the new Empire of Sokoto reorganized the entire area of Hausaland. At first, many disputes arose among various military commanders and Muslim scholars trying to administer the newly-won, widespread territories. When the great shaykh or Shehu Uthman retired to teach and write in 1812, judging these disputes was divided between his brother Abdullahi, installed as the Emir of Gwandu, and Muhammed Bello. Uthman dan Fodio fell ill in 1815 and died in 1817, at which point his son, Muhammed Bello, succeeded to the office of caliph. Soon after this point, the title of Khalifa, or Caliph, seems to have been replaced with the title of "commander of the faithful, or of the Muslims," which in Arabic is *Amir al-mu'minin* and in Hausa, *Sarkin Musulmi*. The title of Sultan for the ruler was commonly used for Muhammed Bello and his successors.

By 1820, the Caliphate or Sultanate of Sokoto comprised seven major emirates, with ten more in the process of being formed. The emirs were selected on the basis of Muslim piety as well as on their original leadership in the jihad. There were two centers of power in the empire: at Gwandu and at Sokoto. While the Caliph or Sultan, now Muhammed Bello, was the political leader of the state, the Emir of Gwandu was respected for piety and religious leadership. Some of the western emirates were administered from Gwandu, but the larger and more important eastern emirates, such as Kano and Katsina, were subordinate directly to Sokoto.

This system depended upon the personal relationship between the caliph and the Emir of Gwandu, and their relationships with the individual emirs. In practice, these relationships among old comrades-in-arms and fellow students seemed to work very well. Muhammed Bello's uncle did not appear to have ambitions to challenge the caliph for supremacy. Most emirs exercised significant independent authority within their realms. During the middle part of the nineteenth century, despite some continued raids and campaigns, the caliphate remained a region of relative peace and prosperity. The empire provided the framework which allowed the British to apply their famous "indirect rule" during their colonial reign.

## Summary

The nineteenth century was thus a time of upheaval and change as all the regions of West Africa, except Liberia, moved toward colonial status to follow the subsequent European conquests at the end of the century. The West African slave trade had developed over a period of several previous centuries and directly involved many coastal peoples and states, including those in Nigeria. Benin and Oyo, especially through its subordinate state of Dahomey, were at times much involved in this trade as were the small trading city-states south of the Igbo homeland in Eastern Nigeria. The British efforts at suppressing the slave trade led to their own increasing presence along the coast in the nineteenth century, especially following the establishment of the freed-slave colony of Sierre Leone. This presence led to increasing British involvement in internal affairs of various African states along the coast.

Map G shows how European influence began to penetrate Africa during the nineteenth century. Note the growing presence of the British along the West African coast. The expansion of the Empire of Sokoto is shown in the interior of the area that became Nigeria. Note that throughout much of the African continent, this century was a period of growing insecurity and destabilization.

[See Map G. The Opening Up and Destabilization of Africa, Mid-19th Century.]

Also in the nineteenth century people in the interior, savanna regions of Northern Nigeria experienced the great Fulani jihads, launched by the outstanding Muslim leader and scholar, Uthman dan Fodio. As a result of this series of jihads, a theocratic Muslim empire ruled over by people now referred to as Hausa-Fulani, dominated much of the area of modern-day Northern Nigeria.

By the beginning of the colonial period at the end of the nineteenth century, the area of modern Nigeria was divided between a Muslim North and an increasingly unstable South, rent by the Yoruba wars in the Southwest, the decline of the slave trading city-states of the Niger Delta and coast, and new and destabilizing influences from traders and missionaries in the Igbo heartland. A new group of Africans with Western-style education and cultural affinities, many of them descendants of slaves freed as a result of the British anti-slavery patrols, had appeared along the coast from Sierre Leone to Lagos, southern Yorubaland, and the Niger Delta region.

## Notes

1 Catherine Coquery-Vidrovitch, *Africa: Endurance and Change South of the Sahara*, trans. David Maisel. Los Angeles: UCLA Press, 1988, pp. 19–20.

2 Robert W. July, *A History of the African People*, New York: Charles Scribners, 1970, p. 271.

3 Mervyn Hiskett, *The Development of Islam in West Africa*, London and New York: Longman, 1984, pp. 130–131.

# THE COLONIAL PERIOD

## Introduction

While European influence continued to grow during the nineteenth century along the coasts, most of the African continent remained independent well into the 1880s. Here and there, European powers had established imperial control over relatively small areas. The British had taken over the former Dutch colony in South Africa, leading some of the Dutch settlers to retreat further into the interior of southern Africa. The French had established a colony in Senegal on the far western coast and were beginning to probe up the Senegal River toward the Western Sudan. These cases represented exceptions, however; for the most part, there were only scattered consuls or posts, like the British colony at Lagos or their post at Elmina or the colony at Freetown, Sierra Leone.

## The European Scramble for Africa

Suddenly, in about the last fifteen years of the century, nearly the entire continent was carved up by European states into protectorates and colonies.[1] By the start of our century, the map of Africa was painted in the red of Great Britain, the green of France, and other imperial colors. Where there formerly had been no European presence in 1880, there was by the end of the century the Belgian Congo, French West Africa, German East Africa, and so on. Only the empire of Ethiopia in the northeast and the Republic of Liberia in the far west remained independent. The acquisition of all this colonial territory went so quickly that observers called it a land scramble—the "Scramble for Africa."

Most important of the many factors leading to this scramble was international rivalry among the powers of Europe. For the most part, the territories in Africa were seized not for their own sake but to forestall other European nations' claims. Certainly there were hopes that some of the colonies would provide minerals or other products that would add to the wealth of the imperial power, but material interests were usually a secondary consideration.

What factors lay behind the urge for empire in nineteenth century Europe? Germany and Italy became unified states for the first time and began to compete for resources from Africa and Asia. The energetic new King of the Belgians, Leopold II, looked for a colonial empire as a way to enhance the prosperity and prestige of his small nation. France, following her defeat by the newly united Germany in 1870 and smarting from Britain's dominance over the Suez Canal, became more aggressive in pushing for empire. All these powers carried their ambitions and rivalries into the African arena.

Leopold hired the famous explorer, Henry Morton Stanley, to make treaties with African rulers along the Congo River and to develop a land and water transport system in the Congo Basin. French officers began signing treaties with Africans north of the Congo River in competition with Leopold's agents. Meanwhile, along the lower Niger River, Sir George Goldie Taubman had organized all the British traders (and driven out the competition) by setting up a chartered company, further extending British influence in the area.

Matters came to a head in 1883–1885 when the leader of the new German Empire, Chancellor Bismarck, became involved, declaring protectorates over far-flung parts of the African continent. Presumably, Bismarck intended to use his African acquisitions as leverage to gain influence in intra-European politics. The British could not fail to notice that each new German dependency was located in an area of Africa of significant concern to British interests—in East Africa, in South Africa, as well as in West Africa. In this latter region, Germany proclaimed a protectorate over Togoland, right next door to recent British acquisitions along the Gold Coast. Also, the Germans announced a huge protectorate over the area of Cameroon adjacent to the Niger Delta region, long within the British sphere of influence.

With the Belgians in the middle of the continent, the French forcing their way into the West African Sudan, and the Germans pushing toward Lake Chad, the race was on. The Portuguese, who long had claimed control of the mouth of the Congo River, protested the sudden entrance of the Germans, French, and Belgians into that area. To avert war among the European states (but with no effort to prevent war with African peoples), an international conference was arranged at Berlin for the winter of 1884–85 to work out an "orderly" process for European acquisition of African territories.

The ostensible purpose of the Berlin Conference was to set up rules allowing for free trade along the Niger and Congo Rivers. Although the final act of the Conference gave lip service to free trade, the practical result was to recognize the primacy of the British on the Niger and the primacy of the new entity, the Congo Free State of Leopold II, on the Congo River. Of more importance for Africans was the provision of the final agreement requiring those European powers claiming territory in Africa to guarantee "effective occupation." While by mutual agreement this requirement could be ignored or minimized, the "effective occupation" clause did motivate European governments to put their people, usually soldiers and administrators, on the ground, especially in disputed areas.

Following the Berlin Conference, Goldie's Niger Company was granted a royal charter giving the company political authority over areas where its agents had signed appropriate treaties with local African leaders. The use of private companies with royal charters had become standard practice for the expansion of British influence. For example, Cecil Rhodes organized the British South Africa Company to extend British control over resources in Southern Africa, especially the diamond-producing area. Such companies provided the capital and people for taking over large areas in return for rights to exploit the resources for profit. A century earlier, the British had used a similar vehicle to take over the vast sub-continent of India. Now in Nigeria, the Royal Niger Company became the mechanism for British imperialism.

The British occupation of Nigeria proceeded in four over-lapping stages between 1885 and about 1905 or 1906. First, they forestalled French ambitions in Yorubaland and extended control over the warring Yoruba kingdoms. Second, the forces of the Royal Niger Company subdued the Fulani emirates of the north. Third, the British continued to eliminate the resistance of the Niger delta trading city-states within the Oil Rivers Protectorate. Finally, the British embarked on a series of "pacification" campaigns to bring the Igbo hinterland under their control. The village-based societies of the Igbo were the last areas to be subdued. Partly because of the fragmented political systems, it was necessary to conquer this region—almost village by village. We turn now to a brief description of each of these stages.

The lands of the Yoruba people were torn by nearly continuous warfare throughout the nineteenth century. These internal wars were the result of the break-up of the old empire of Oyo and the efforts of new Yoruba centers to seize power and trading advantage. As sources of slaves and other trade were cut off, in the north by the Fulani jihad states and in the south by the antislavery efforts of the British, the Oyo empire lost much of its economic base. Internal weaknesses became evident following the reign of Alafin Abiodun, who had had to deal with his over-powerful Bashorun, Gaha. The army seemed to lose its effectiveness and cohesion from this time. External factors hastening disintegration included Fulani attacks from the North and the assertion of independence and hostility by the Dahomean Empire to the West. With the fall of Ilorin to the jihadists and its virtual incorporation into the Empire of Sokoto, Oyo (that is, Oyo Ile, or the original Oyo, city) was mostly cut off from its provinces to the south as well as from access to lucrative trade. Various tributary cities began to exercise their independence, and the Oyo armies were defeated in a series of battles as they struggled to maintain control over the empire. Oyo soldiers fighting in the south found that they could not return home to the northern areas by that time dominated by the Emirate of Ilorin and so became wandering military bands in search of new homes. After the final defeat of Oyo by Ilorin in 1835 and the death of the Alafin as a result of that defeat, the ancient city of Oyo was abandoned and her people migrated to the South where the forested areas provided more protection from marauding Fulani cavalry. A new Oyo was established in the South (the current Oyo that appears on modern maps) and the new, powerful city-states of Ibadan and Abeokuta were established by people dislocated by these forced migrations.

As the Oyo empire began to disintegrate, there were outbreaks of fighting throughout Yorubaland. The British, in their efforts at ending the slave trade and reestablishing order for traders and missionaries, found themselves increasingly involved in internal Yoruba affairs. Remember that the colony at Lagos was established when the British Consul from the Oil Rivers became involved in a dispute about the ruler of Lagos and the troubles of the mission station at Abeokuta.

The major expedition leading to the occupation of Yorubaland was a British-led invasion to open the roads between Lagos and the Yoruba city of Ijebu-Ode. The Ijebu and their Egba allies (whose city was Abeokuta) had refused to allow open trade through their territory to Ibadan. In May of 1892 a force of over 450 men, consisting mostly of Hausa and West Indians but which also included 100 men sent from Ibadan, started north from Lagos. This British-led force was well-equipped with modern rifles, cannon, one machine gun, and some rocket launchers. The Ijebu army of about 10,000 men which opposed this force was defeated, sustaining heavy casualties. The Ijebu and Egba Yoruba quickly made peace, and the rest of the Yoruba rulers signed treaties with the British. One of the ruling officials of the Ijebu, the Balogun, almost immediately became a supporter of British rule as well as a convert to Islam. One of the main festivals in Ijebu-Ode to this day is *Ileya* (from the Muslim festival called *'Id al-Kabir*), which recalls early parades of Muslim Yoruba and Hausa-Fulani supporters of this ruler in the early 1900s.[2] In this case the outside forces represented by the British and Islam came together in the chaotic conditions of turn-of-the-century Yorubaland.

The British next turned their attention to the north, to the Caliphate of Sokoto. The Royal Niger Company had earlier concluded a treaty with the Caliph, which the company interpreted as giving them a protectorate over the empire of the caliphate. The Caliph, on the other hand, considered that he had merely granted the company a monopoly on European trade within his lands. In 1897, the company moved against two of the southernmost emirates, Ilorin and Nupe, and defeated them. In 1899, however, the British government took over the property of the company, withdrawing the charter but paying a handsome indemnity to the stockholders. In 1900, under Lugard, the British undertook to enforce "effective occupation" of the domains of Sokoto and the state of Borno.

Lugard's task in northern Nigeria was daunting. Most of his forces had been sent to fight a war against the Ashanti in the Gold Coast, and yet he was called on to establish an administration over a territory in the north containing at least 15 million people. It is no wonder that it took most of the period of 1900 to 1906 to complete the conquest.

One of the first emirates to fall was the relatively new state of Kontagora, a notorious slaving center taken in the year 1900. Some important cities, like Zaria, gave in without a fight in the face of superior British armaments. Kano, however, required a major expedition in 1902. As the largest and most important city, Kano was central to the British strategy. The British force was again quite small, 772 African soldiers and 36 British officers, but equipped with cannon and machine guns. When this force reached Kano, the cannon succeeded in battering down the wall at one point, which allowed the city to be taken easily, although the palace was hotly defended. Another force returning from Sokoto attacked the British, but the typical Fulani cavalry charge was utterly ineffective against the British weapons.

The British then attacked Sokoto and defeated the army of the new caliph, Attahiru. A final 1906 uprising at Sokoto against the British was crushed when the newly appointed caliph backed the British.

The third part of the British occupation of Nigeria involved minor but troublesome expeditions in the Niger Delta area. Although the British influence would seem to have been more long-standing in this area of the Oil Rivers Protectorate (re-named the Niger Coast Protectorate in 1893) than in other regions of Nigeria, there continued to be pockets of resistance. First, west of the Delta the British had to send one expedition against a ruler blocking the Benin River in 1894, and a more famous expedition against the still-independent city of Benin in 1897. As was the case with Ijebu in Yorubaland, the ruler (or Oba) of Benin refused to allow free trade through his domains. The British claimed as a second cause for war the Oba's continuation of extensive human sacrifice. When the acting Consul-General for the British was killed in Benin on a peaceful visit in January 1897, hostilities ensued. The British set out in February and, tragically, the Oba resorted to human sacrifices throughout the city in an effort to generate ritual power to defeat the British. The city was looted of its artistic treasures—the Benin bronzes and ivory carvings—and the Oba was deported. Similar fates were meted out to recalcitrant rulers of the Delta city-states.

The military phase of the occupation of the interior of Igboland lasted longer than that of other areas of Nigeria—from roughly 1900 to as late as 1910—although some scattered opposition continued until World War I. The British had to defeat armies and skilled warriors piece-meal in each town, village, or village-group. The dense forest terrain worked to the disadvantage of the colonial forces, as well. The first major expedition was mounted against the Aro-Chukwu because of their continued association with slaving in the Delta area. The campaign took nearly six months, from July through December of 1901, before the British were able to enter the central town of the Aro-Chukwu and burn the shrine and image of the famous oracle.

Following the establishment of the African colonies, Europeans and Americans accepted the idea that the imposition of colonial rule on the Africans had been for the most part peaceful and even welcomed by African peoples. This brief summary of the British conquest of Nigeria indicates, however, that there was armed resistance. In many parts of Nigeria and throughout Africa, the conquest, while small-scale by standards of European warfare, was violent and deadly.

## The Colonial System in Nigeria

Some have said that the British empire in Africa, like those of other European nations, was acquired in a fit of absent-mindedness. Once the colonies were secured, the Europeans were less than certain about what do with them. The first phase of colonialism, as we have seen, involved a gradual extension of authority over the people and territory. Map H shows how the continent was divided by the beginning of this century. The British had huge territories in eastern and southern Africa, while the French controlled vast territories in West Africa. The British colonies in West Africa, however, were by and large the richest in resources and the most populous.

[See Map H. The Map Completed, c. 1902.]

The British had not acquired their colonies with the idea of creating any tax burdens on the British people, and so the colonies had to be inexpensive to administer and, it was hoped, self-supporting in a very short time. Direct government grants were used to pay for the "pacification," that is, the military campaigns to put down resistance, and for the beginnings of an infrastructure like new roads and railways.

The second phase of colonialism was marked by efforts to develop economic self-sufficiency in the colonies. Three methods were available to the colonial governments in Africa. First, they could induce the African farmers to grow "cash crops," crops for sale on the international market, rather than subsistence crops. Second, they could encourage European settlers to go out to the colonies to hire Africans to work on farms or in mines for them. Third, they could turn over to private companies the rights to exploit mineral or agricultural wealth in an area, in exchange for private financing for building roads, railways, and the like. The unifying purpose was to bring the Africans into a cash-based economy so that they could be taxed to support the colonial administration. A second purpose was to make the Africans consumers of manufactured goods from the European country, paid for with the new cash wages. Africa, in turn, was to export products such as copper, ivory, rubber, palm oil, coffee, and cocoa for European consumption.

In West Africa, and in Nigeria in particular, a market in cash crops and commodities had grown up even prior to the colonial period. This fact, coupled with climatic conditions unhealthy for European settlers, helped determine that cash crops grown by African farmers would be the basic method for economic development in West Africa. The Niger Delta of southeastern Nigeria was already one of the leading areas in the world for the export of palm products. In Yorubaland, cocoa became the most important product. In the north, the major cash crops were groundnuts (peanuts) and cotton.

To facilitate the expansion of these cash crops and their export, the colony had to develop a new transportation system. Beginning at Lagos in 1898, the British colonial government succeeded in constructing a rail line all the way to Kano by 1912. New harbor facilities had to be dredged at Lagos and at the new city of Port Harcourt, near the mouth of the Niger. By 1920 a second major railroad extended from Port Harcourt north through Igboland on up to Zaria where it intersected with the Kano line. Typically in West Africa, lines of communication and transportation run from the coast to the interior, north-south, while east-west connections are few. Colonial governments developed communications systems which suited colonial interests—getting products out of the interior to be exported at the coast.

The colonial administration of Nigeria was based upon the philosophy of "Indirect Rule" as worked out by Frederick Lugard in his years in Northern Nigeria. While indirect rule had been the basis for some British colonial administration in India and elsewhere,

Lugard developed the idea much more systematically as the fundamental principle of colonial administration.[3]

As the term implies, "indirect rule" involves maintaining the traditional rulers as functionaries ultimately answerable to an outside authority. The emirs of Northern Nigeria were ideal candidates for such a system, since they already appeared to function as governors for the Caliph of Sokoto at the time of the conquest. With each emir, Lugard placed a British Resident whose function was to advise the emir in his administration. The term "Resident" was intended to imply that the British administrator was merely "in residence" with the emir, rather than a superior to the emir. In fact, the Resident directed the local ruler who effectively became part of the British administration. The Resident was to assure that the dignity and trappings associated with the traditional rulers were maintained, however. In Northern Nigeria this policy meant that Islam would be protected; Christian missions were therefore officially excluded from the north. The British saw themselves as replacing the Caliphate in supervising the emirs. Although the British political officers were supposed to help "modernize" emirate administration, in practice they saw their function as preserving old customs and practices.

This system seemed to work so well among the emirates in Northern Nigeria that Lugard tried to extend it throughout the colony. As Governor-General, Lugard was in overall control of the government with the assistance of two lieutenant-governors, one for Northern Nigeria, the other for Southern Nigeria. This decision had the unfortunate result of maintaining a north-south division in Nigeria that troubles the politics of the nation to this day.

The effort to implement indirect rule in the south was much less successful than it had been among the northern emirates. While the system might be practicable for Benin where the Oba had powers similar to the emirs, it was less so among the Yoruba where the power of rulers like the Alafin was much more limited. During the First World War, uprisings in parts of Yorubaland occurred when people felt that newly appointed rulers exceeded the traditional authority of their office.

Among the small-scale societies of the Igbo, the system was especially difficult to implement. The British decided to subdivide African polities, designating some "advanced" and others "primitive."

The "primitive" areas were those which appeared to be stateless—the small-scale, democratic societies like those of the Igbo. Critics in England and elsewhere had to wonder at a system that termed emirates advanced and democratic systems primitive.

To introduce indirect rule among the Igbo and other similarly organized peoples, the British used a system of "warrant chiefs." Likely candidates from among the elders or respected leaders of a village were made chiefs by "warrant." These warrant chiefs then sat on a Native Council which performed both executive and judicial functions. This method of forcing indirect rule on areas where it was inappropriate is satirized in the novel, *Arrow of God,* by Chinua Achebe. The protagonist, Ezeulu, is offered the warrant chieftaincy for his Igbo village by the local British district commissioner. The commissioner is puzzled and irritated when Ezeulu turns down this "honor." Often, the position of warrant chief went to one of the "new men," those who prospered as traders or functionaries in the new regime but did not meet traditional criteria for leadership. These "new men" were widely resented among the Igbo.

## The Consequences of Indirect Rule

If indirect rule had clear benefits for the British (it was economical, efficient, and generally effective), its benefits to the Africans were fewer. Although indirect rule was perhaps less disruptive and less brutal than direct foreign control would have been, the negative consequences were many. The most damaging were those that altered the internal control mechanisms of traditional society. For example, indirect rule often perpetuated the control of corrupt or autocratic rulers who were "frozen in" during a time of great political and economic change in the country. Newly educated African elites, ironically, were "frozen out" by the same system which had no use for fresh and vigorous African leadership. These young elites, educated as lawyers, doctors, teachers, and other professionals, found few outlets for their political aspirations. Finally, indirect rule ignored the political realities of small-scale societies, preferring instead to twist that reality to fit the Lugardian mold.

The colonial period in Nigeria, as in most of Africa, proved a brief but a highly significant interlude. Over a period of sixty years, the new nation of Nigeria was created where no such entity had existed before. The early stages of the colonial administration

(1905–1920) saw the development of the infrastructure necessary to the modern nation-state—roads, harbors, railroads, bridges.

This infrastructure was the first important element in the change toward a new Nigeria. In the early stages of road-building, much of the construction was done by forced labor, with African villages required to provide labor in lieu of taxes. These roads created new markets and commercial possibilities and made it possible for Africans to travel far and wide. The Igbo especially spread from southeast Nigeria throughout the country as traders and government workers.

A second element, the creation of a cash economy, probably had already started among the trading cities of Nigeria and was a major early effect of the colonial period. The necessity to pay taxes in the form of money was an early impetus to the system. The development of cash crops and rural and urban paid labor followed. The cash economy also created interest in European manufactured products unknown in Africa before colonial times—bicycles, radios, and European-style clothing.

Third, the colonial period saw the growth of African cities and towns. Lagos became a metropolitan area: Kano, now a railroad terminus, more than tripled in size. New towns like Port Harcourt sprang up and quickly grew into cities. Within the cities, ethnic identities became even more important than they had been in the countryside as newcomers looked for familiar ways and languages to help ease them into the milieu of the strange, large city, which brought together people from many different ethnic and linguistic backgrounds.

A fourth important effect lay in the development of an institutionalized or "Westernized" education system. Throughout southern Nigeria, the schools were associated with the Christian missions so that there was a connection between obtaining a "modern" education and conversion to the new faith. Such an educational system, of course, had an effect in undermining the traditional bases for age groups and initiation ceremonies that had constituted the educational system in earlier times.

**Table 3. PRINCIPAL NIGERIAN CITIES ESTIMATED POPULATION BY 1975**

| City | Population | Ethnic Region* |
|---|---|---|
| Lagos (then federal capital) | 1,060,848 | Yoruba, Edo |
| Ibadan | 847,000 | Yoruba |
| Ogbomosho | 432,000 | Yoruba |
| Kano | 399,000 | Hausa-Fulani |
| Oshogbo | 282,000 | Yoruba |
| Ilorin | 282,000 | Yoruba, Hausa-Fulani |
| Abeokuta | 253,000 | Egba Yoruba |
| Port Harcourt | 242,000 | Igbo, Ijo |
| Zaria | 224,000 | Hausa-Fulani |
| Ilesha | 224,000 | Yoruba |
| Onitsha | 220,000 | Igbo |
| Iwo | 214,000 | Yoruba |
| Ado-Ekiti | 213,000 | Yoruba |
| Kaduna | 202,000 | Hausa-Fulani |
| Enugu | 187,000 | Igbo |
| Ife | 176,000 | Yoruba |
| Oyo (new Oyo) | 152,000 | Yoruba |
| Benin City | 136,000 | Edo (Bini) |

*All cities today are quite ethnically mixed; this designation reflects the historical or regional identification of the modern city. Source: *Africa South of the Sahara,* 1994, 23rd ed. London: Europa Publications, Ltd., p. 670.

In politics, a fifth effect was the tendency of colonial administration to undermine traditional systems of governance. It was obvious that traditional rulers were no longer independent or sovereign; they were clearly taking orders from the British colonial administrators. A related effect was the realization of some African unity as a result of common treatment by colonial authorities. African suddenly became conscious of a new shared identity, became aware that they were all Africans, in contradistinction to the white colonial officials and missionaries who were not. Gradually the goal of African political awareness became to win rights: first within the colonial system, and eventually as part of an effort to take over the existing colonial structures. Thus, the colonial state became the basis for future political action.

## Summary

The colonial period in West Africa was ushered in by the Europeans' Scramble for Africa occasioned by rivalries among European powers more than intrinsic interest in African territories themselves. Nigeria fell to the British, thus bringing to closure a long period of growing British involvement in African affairs along the Nigerian coast and up the Niger River. The conquest was not always peaceful or nonviolent, although it was usually depicted as such in popular British and even American thought.

Following the rapid carving up of the African map, the European colonial powers were somewhat unsure what to do next. Once in power, the British adopted the policy of "indirect rule" for their African colonies, on the model developed by Lord Lugard after his occupation of Northern Nigeria for the Royal Niger Company. Because Nigeria's climate and disease environment was not conducive to British settlement there, the colonial officials encouraged the Africans to grow cash crops in order to earn currency with which they could pay taxes to meet the expenses of the colonial administration.

The colonial period in Nigeria was relatively brief—much briefer, for example, than the British occupation of the colonies that became the United States of America. Major changes took place during this 60 to 70 years, however. A new infrastructure of roads, railroads, harbors, bridges, and improved waterways provided for easier movement of goods and people. This infrastructure made it easier for the colonial powers to extract natural resources and crops from Nigeria and allowed for easier movement of people from rural areas to new towns and cities. During this period the Igbo people, particularly, spread out throughout the new colony, serving as shopkeepers, clerks, soldiers, police, and in other positions made possible by the new colonial administration. Especially in the new urban areas, ethnic identities became more important and divisive than they had been before. As a result, large groups such as Igbo, Yoruba, and Hausa-Fulani developed an ethnic consciousness beyond the scope of earlier times. The colonial government preferred to categorize peoples by simple, large ethnic identities, and such categories took on lives of their own with consequences that will be seen in the final two chapters.

## Notes

1 A protectorate falls under the Foreign Office of a European government—the European state has extended its official protection over an area that is still nominally independent; a colony is administered under a Colonial Office and is considered directly under the control of the imperial state. In the British system, the protectorates were further from the coast or capital and gradually converted to integral parts of the colonies.

2 J. D. Y. Peel, "Historicity and Pluralism in Some Recent Studies in Yoruba Religion," *Africa*, 64 (1994), 153.

3 Retiring from colonial service in 1919, Lugard published his principles of indirect rule in the book, *The Dual Mandate for Tropical Africa*, which became a basic manual for British colonial administration throughout Africa.

# THE GROWTH OF AFRICAN NATIONALISM

The establishment of colonial governments in Africa was immediately followed by political movements intended to influence and eventually to end the colonial regimes. Gradually, the goal of these movements was to replace the white colonial officials with African presidents and parliamentarians presiding over the new states within artificially created borders. In Nigeria, even more than in many other African colonies, this development of African nationalism was complicated by the powerful allegiances based on regionalism, religion, and newly significant ethnic identities.

## Early Stages of African Nationalism

Nationalism in Africa can be understood as passing through several stages. The first stage, as we have seen, was resistance to the European occupation and to the changes it imposed on Africans. The goal was not to create a new nation, but to restore the African state, empire, or village society that had existed before the coming of the imperial forces. In the second stage, Africans from different ethnic groups developed notions of general protest, cutting across traditional and ethnic lines. Racial discrimination, forced labor, taxation, and general lack of African representation in their own government all were objects of protest. The third stage was represented by political movements or parties often begun by a small, Western-educated class among the Africans. These movements went beyond resistance or protest. The end in view was the creation of a new nation based on Western democratic models and within colonially drawn borders. In the fourth stage, political mobilization extended to the masses.

Important social and cultural change typically develops in the wake of intellectual antecedents. Those antecedents most significant in shaping African nationalism in West Africa include the Freetown Creole elites from Sierra Leone such as Samuel Ajayi Crowther, the first African bishop in West Africa, and James Africanus Beale Horton, the Igbo educated at Fourah Bay College. Horton espoused two important principles: first, that there were no physical or intellectual differences between Africans and Europeans; and, second, that the process of social improvement he saw occurring along the West African coast in the middle 1800s was destined to end in the establishment of free African nations.

Another important intellectual precursor of African nationalism, Edward Wilmot Blyden, became editor of the first newspaper in Liberia, *The Liberia Herald*, in the 1850s and became a renowned professor of classics at Liberia College. Blyden, who was probably of Hausa background, believed that each race had its own particular assets to contribute to the well-being of all people. Africans, therefore, should not try to copy or become Europeans. There was a distinct African personality or consciousness. Blyden's concept of "Africanness" was based on three principles: (1) the concept of community—that Africans placed a special emphasis on human community and interpersonal relations; (2) consonance with nature—that Africans lived in better harmony with their world than did the Europeans; and (3) communion with God—an unusually strong spiritual strength permeates traditional African cultures.

The Pan-African Movement represented another antecedent to African nationalism. At the end of World War I, the American sociologist and founder of the NAACP, William Edward Burghardt DuBois revived the Pan-African idea and organized a congress to meet in Paris during the Versailles Peace Conference in an effort to bring before the delegates the needs of the African peoples. The African representative of the French government from Senegal, Blaise Diagne, was instrumental in persuading the French government to allow the meeting, largely because Diagne had raised thousands of West African troops to fight in the trenches for France in World War I and so had some real influence with the French.

Subsequent Pan-African Congresses were held in 1921 (London, Brussels, Paris), in 1923 (London and Lisbon), and again in 1926–27 in London. The platform of this early Pan-African Movement seems quite moderate by today's standards: a code of international law applicable to all colonial territories; a recognition that African land was held in trust for the future benefit of Africans rather than for white settlers; regulations on the development of capitalism in Africa; the abolition of slavery, forced labor, and capital punishment in the colonies; increased education for the African people; and progressive growth in African participation in colonial governments.

The Fifth and final Pan-African Congress was held in London at the end of World War II, still under the presidency of W.E.B. DuBois. By that time, the outcome of the war, with the exhaustion of the colonial powers (France, England, Belgium) and the rise to world power of two anti- or at least non-colonial superpowers, gave hope that the end of colonial rule in Africa was in sight. Prominent in this Congress were many of the first generation of leaders of the new states that became independent in Africa over the following fifteen years. The Pan-African Congress, therefore, provided inspiration and leadership for the growth of nationalism throughout the continent during the first half of the century.

## The Nationalist Movement in Nigeria

In Nigeria, the first major nationalist stirrings were among the educated classes in Lagos. The Lagos nationalists maintained a campaign against the policies of Lord Lugard, especially those of the amalgamation of Southern and Northern Nigeria and the accompanying expansion of indirect rule to the South. During the period around World War I this opposition was spearheaded by Thomas H. Jackson, the editor of *The Lagos Weekly Herald*. The early nationalist program attacked the racial arrogance of the British on the one hand, while it called for the institution of British parliamentary style politics on the other. It championed Western educated Africans as those most fit to run a modern state, but opposed the growing disrespect for traditional institutions.

A dispute involving traditional rulers brought to the fore the leading nationalist of the 1920s: Herbert Macaulay (or HM, as he was known to his followers). When the British high-handedly replaced the ruling Eleko with another, Macaulay's group spearheaded a protest which lasted until 1933 when a new governor restored the original ruler to his position. Already mobilized over this issue, Macaulay's group responded quickly when the colonial government decided to allow Lagos to elect three members to a newly expanded Legislative Council. (LegCo, as it was called, served in an advisory capacity to the governor; there were 46 members, 27 of them administration bureaucrats; only 4 were elected.) Jackson and Macaulay organized a political party, the Nigerian National Democratic Party (NNDP) to contest the elections.

Both Jackson and Macaulay were part of a Westernized class occasionally referred to as Saro along the English-speaking West African coast, many of them descendants of the "re-captives" settled at Freetown, Sierre Leone, by the anti-slavery patrols of the early nineteenth century. Mostly of Yoruba and Igbo descent like Crowther and Horton, the Saro looked to Western, especially British, models for their political and social ideals. A group of professionals—lawyers, medical doctors, teachers, and journalist—these Saro tended to live in the non-traditional new cities of the coast such as Freetown, Cape Coast and Accra (in modern-day Ghana), and Lagos. These people were ambivalent in their feelings about traditional rulers and culture. Having been educated in Britain or British-style colleges, they saw traditionalists as old-fashioned and backward, inadequate to the tasks of running a modern nation-state. On the other hand, as the case of the Eleko shows, they felt the need to express solidarity with Africans in disputes with the colonial authorities. Their dilemma highlights one of the political problems engendered by Britain's policy of indirect rule.

The NNDP successfully elected their candidates to the unofficial seats on the LegCo from 1923 until 1938. Such a small number of elected members could have very little influence over the course of government policy, and this lack of real power became the source for further frustration. The NNDP represents the third stage of nationalism described above, a party of mostly Westernized, educated Africans. This group was challenged in the late 1930s by the growth of a more militant brand of nationalism, represented by one of the great leaders of Nigerian and, indeed, African nationalism, Nnamdi Azikiwe (known as Zik). Azikiwe, an Igbo, was educated at Lincoln College in Pennsylvania. When he returned to Nigeria in the 1930s, he became a journalist and newspaper owner. As editor of *The West African Pilot,* he led the attack on colonial abuses. In 1938 he became a force in the recently organized Nigerian Youth Movement, which challenged the older NNDP. In 1941, Azikiwe took the lead in organizing 101 "tribal" unions into a new, much larger political group, the National Council of Nigeria and the Cameroons, the NCNC. (After World War I, German Kamerun had been divided into two League of Nations mandate territories under Britain and France; the British Cameroons were adjacent to eastern Nigeria.) As a gesture toward unity among the nationalists, Macaulay was named president, while Azikiwe held the important post of Executive Secretary.

World War II was a watershed in the development of African nationalism and the movement toward the independence of the African colonies. Both Great Britain and France were significantly weakened by the war, and the two superpowers that emerged following the war, the United States and the Soviet Union, were not colonial powers nor were they sympathetic to the maintaining of European colonies in Africa. Map I shows the situation on the African continent as the final push toward independence began at the close of the war.

[See Map I. Colonial Africa between the Two World Wars.]

At the close of World War II, in which Nigerian troops fought in the Asian theater of operations, the British introduced a new constitution for Nigeria. The NCNC launched a series of protests against this constitution because it continued to give preference to traditional authorities despite the growing political presence of urban and mass-based parties; in other words, it perpetuated indirect rule. During these years, however, the NCNC began to lose its radical image as local branches came under increasing control by teachers, businessmen, and other moderate elements.

Meanwhile, large political parties began to take shape in other parts of the colony, which the British had by this time reorganized into three administrative regions: the Northern Region, comprising roughly half of Nigeria; the Eastern Region, including the heartland of the Igbo; and the Western Region, home of the Yoruba. This three-part division was to have significant consequences on political developments.

In the north, the area of the Hausa-Fulani emirates, political organizations were based more on traditional ruling elites than was the case in the south. One of the leading figures in this development was Abubakar Tafewa Balewa, destined to become the first Prime Minister of independent Nigeria. Born into a family of small office-holders under the ruler of Bauchi, he was sent to college to receive a Western education. He graduated from Katsina College and became headmaster of an elementary school. (Many of the earlier nationalists came from the ranks of either journalism or teaching.) After completing a degree in London in 1945–46, he was appointed to the Emir's Council, an advisory body in Northern Nigeria. Although he spoke out against corruption and inefficiency of these "Native Authorities," he stopped short of calling for their abolition. Balewa was involved in forming the major political party of the north, the Northern People's Congress, or the NPC.

Two other Northerners were important in these early stages of party politics. From the ruling house of Sokoto, Ahmadu Bello, better known in Nigerian politics as the Sardauna of Sokoto, became head of the NPC. Aminu Kano, who represented a more liberal trend in northern politics, came from the patrician class of Fulani scholars. Kano, like Balewa, was educated in a local college and in London. He was favorably impressed by the British Labour Party and tended to support the interests of workers and urban migrants. When the Sardauna of Sokoto made the NPC a caucus for the traditional Hausa-Fulani ruling elites, he forced Kano out of the party. The latter went on to form and head his own party, the Northern Elements Progressive Union. The 1950 manifesto of this party clearly shows that the Hausa-Fulani of the North should not be seen as a monolithic political grouping:

> All parties are but the expression of class interests, and as the interest of the Talakawa ("commoners" in Hausa) is diametrically opposed to the interests of all sections of the master class [Hausa-Fulani rulers and supporters], the party seeking the emancipation of the Talakawa must naturally be hostile to the party of the oppressors.[1]

In the southwest of the colony, the Western Region, another new leader came to the fore in the late forties, Obafemi Awolowo. Awolowo had been a chief in the colonial administration, a successful cocoa grower and businessman. In 1950, while the NPC was gathering strength in the north, he formed the Action Group (AG), relying on the support of Yoruba professionals, businessmen, and some of the Obas. This new political organization grew out of a Yoruba cultural organization, the *Egbe Omo Oduduwa*, which had been formed in 1948. The non-Yoruba elements in the region began to look to the NCNC for support, fearing domination by the AG of the Yoruba. Other groups in the Western Region called for the creation of a Midwestern Region, roughly the area of old Benin, to avoid domination by the Yoruba.

## The Growth of Regionalism during the Colonial Period

Regionalism as a serious obstacle to national unity was inherited from the colonial period. As early as the amalgamation of the northern region (dominated by the Islamic emirates) with the southern region (dominated by the Yoruba in the West and the Igbo in the East) the main lines of fissure appeared. The Southerners tended to look upon the north as backward and potentially threatening; the Northerners in their turn feared the domination of the Southerners. Through a series of constitutions imposed upon their colony the British perpetuated the idea of federalism and separate regional autonomy.

These constitutions represented steps along the way toward the self-government and ultimate independence of Nigeria, but they also hardened the divisions within the new state. The names and details are not as important as the trends these steps represented.

The Clifford Constitution of 1922, named for the governor Sir Hugh Clifford, set up a LegCo (Legislative Council) consisting of 46 members. Of these 46 members, 10 were to be Africans, four of whom were elected (Lagos elected three, while the Cross River region elected one). These elections, the first African elections in British West Africa, started HM, or Herbert Macaulay, on his political career. The Northern Province did not fall under the LegCo, however, but was to continue under indirect rule through the emirates.

The Richards Constitution, immediately following World War II, instituted a LegCo for all of Nigeria; in other words, the north was included for the first time. Although the new LegCo was a bit smaller (45 members versus 46 under the Clifford Constitution) there were now 28 African members. Only four were elected; the other 24 were appointed by the colonial government. The point was, nonetheless, that African representation was increased.

The Richards Constitution was relatively short-lived. A series of local and regional meetings resulted in a national (colonial) conference at Ibadan in 1950. The new constitution, known as the Macpherson Constitution for the then current Colonial Governor, brought in a federal system with three regions favoring the majority ethnic communities in each region (Yoruba in the west, Igbo in the east, and Hausa-Fulani in the north). Regional governments and assemblies made their appearance at this time.

The 1951 constitution, which made governmental ministers heads of departments in the central government has been described as a compromise "aiming to accommodate the hopes of southern modernists and the fears of northern traditionalists.[2] The Secretary of State for the Colonies in London expressed his fear to Macpherson that African ministers in the new national government would feel more loyalty to their regions than to the new nation. In response, Macpherson wrote, "I feel, however, that any such tendency would be quickly corrected by the nature of a Minister's work at the centre. He will have to deal with questions of a Nigeria-wide nature, and also, on occasion, with questions with which his region might not be directly concerned. The effect of this would be to instill into him a Nigerian habit of thought . . ."[3] One result of the new government structure, however, was the rise of regional and ethnically-based political parties that undermined national unity and integration. This result made it clear that Macpherson's reasoning had been far too idealistic.

The reality that brought home the weakness of Macpherson's reasoning was a political uproar within the year when a member of the national legislature introduced a motion calling for independence by 1956. Before independence could be considered, the north demanded even more restrictions on the power of the central government, in order to prevent any tampering by the Southerners with the privileges of the entrenched Hausa-Fulani elite. The new constitution of 1954, the Lyttleton Constitution, provided even more regional autonomy than its predecessor. The judiciary, for example, was regionalized. The institution and role of "customary courts," including Islamic or shari'a courts, were left to each region. The central government was responsible for only defense, foreign affairs, and custom duties. A declaration on fundamental human rights was included at this time as part of an effort to safeguard the rights of minorities in each region. The African assembly of 1954 was dominated by a coalition of the NCNC and the northern party, the Northern Peoples Congress, as together they had a majority of the council of ministers. It was under this constitution that discussions leading to national independence were begun.

In 1957, the year in which Ghana became the first sub-Saharan African colony to gain independence, Nigerians elected their first federal prime minister.[4] In that year, a motion was passed by the Federal House calling for independence by 1959. Great Britain agreed to October of 1960. The elections to determine the national leaders of the new state were held during 1959. The Federal House of Assembly was to have 320 seats allotted as follows: 174 in the North, 73 in the East, and 62 in the West. In addition, there would be 8 in the portion of the UN-mandated territories of the Cameroons that had voted to join Nigeria, and 3 in Lagos, the federal capital. The AG (Action Group) of Awolowo campaigned hard among the ethnic minorities in the East and the North in the hope of undercutting the majority of the NCNC-NPC coalition.

## The Coming of Independence

Clearly, the lines of disunity were in place as the nationalists began to debate the basis for Nigeria's transition to independence. These lines of opposition were reinforced by regional, ideological, ethnic, and religious divisions. The north was dominated by politics of the traditional elite, conservative elements in the NPC whose power had its origins in the policies of Lord Lugard as well as the Sultanate of Sokoto and jihads of Uthman dan Fodio. The Western Region was dominated by the AG of Awolowo, representing the interests of the newly prosperous Westernized elites. In the Eastern Region the more mass-based party of the NCNC, under Azikiwe, was dominant. There were opposition elements in each region as smaller groups feared domination by the larger. The constitution-writing process was delayed through the 1950s by the competition among these points of view. The NCNC favored a more centralized form of government, while other parties held out for a looser, federal type of system that would leave some autonomy to each of the three regions.

By 1959, the nationalists and the British government finally agreed on the new constitution based on regional federalism. As one would expect, the constitution was modeled on the British parliamentary system with the head of the government named by the party holding a majority in the national legislature. When elections were held that year the NPC, representing the most populous part of the country, won the most seats but fell well short of a majority. Given the parliamentary system, the only way a government could be organized was if two or more parties formed a coalition to make a majority. The NPC and NCNC agreed to join in a coalition and formed the first government of Nigeria, with Balewa as Prime Minister and Azikiwe as Governor-General (ceremonial head of state). In this way, Nigeria became independent in October of 1960.

## Summary: Results of the Colonial Period

The roughly sixty years in which Nigeria was a colony had profound effects which are central to an understanding of the contemporary problems of the country. These effects were, for the most part, shared with other African states that had been gobbled up by the imperial scramble. The persistent influence of the colonial period can be seen in the development of a dependent economy and the difficulties of national integration that militated against a strong national identity.

The colonial economy was originally based on the production of a few raw materials for export, mainly to the colonizing power. This type of agricultural economy was based on unskilled labor. Manufacturing and processing sectors remained largely undeveloped or even absent. The capital for the development of these agricultural (and some mining) industries came mostly from overseas, usually from the metropolitan power; in consequence, most of the profits flowed overseas, as well. The public expenditures by the colonial governments, as we have seen, went largely for the development of roads, railways, harbors, and other infrastructure that would facilitate the export of these primary commodities. The funding of education most often was left to philanthropic institutions like missions.

Throughout most of Africa, this kind of economic arrangement resulted in societies with small, literate and skilled elites and a mass of unskilled laborers who spent part of their time in urban areas and part in rural villages. Nigeria may have been better off than many West African colonies in that some farmers, like the cocoa growers, were able to become relatively prosperous. The Eastern Region was also fairly prosperous as industrious Igbo people spread throughout the colony as traders, merchants, clerks, and government employees. The northern region remained relatively less well-developed.

By 1960, the year of Nigerian independence, two-thirds of Africa's exports were agricultural commodities, with cocoa, groundnuts, palm products, coffee, and cotton the most important.

The problem with production of this sort was that whole regions became dependent upon the world markets for a single commodity. When the price for cocoa or palm oil fell, devastating effects ensued for local economies. Furthermore, when an area depended primarily on a single crop the threats of disease, poor weather, insects, and so on were magnified. When food production suffered, newly urbanized populations who could not grow food for themselves suffered disproportionately. Cassava, a cheap product, became extremely important in the Nigerian diet as a result.

National integration also was made more difficult because of colonial policies. Colonies were not created on the basis of traditional ethnic or geographic borders. Within a large colony such as Nigeria, hundreds of different ethnic groups were identified and administered as a single entity. Indirect rule, moreover, favored some ethnic groups above the others. In areas inhabited by several large ethnic groups—the Hausa-Fulani, the Igbo, and the Yoruba of Nigeria, for example—serious conflict was inevitable. Like other new African governments, Nigeria's faced the formidable task of creating a feeling of national unity where neither nation nor unity had existed before.

## Notes

1 Cited in Basil Davidson, *The Black Man's Burden: Africa and the Curse of the Nation-State*, New York: Times Books, 1992, p.109.

2 Ali A. Mazrui and Michael Tidy, *Nationalism and New States in Africa*, Nairobi: Heinemann Press, 1984, p. 93.

3 Correspondence between Sir John Macpherson (Governor) and James Griffiths, Secretary of State for the Colonies, 15 April 1951, Doc. J45 A132, Africana Collection, Boston University.

4 The Republic of the Sudan did gain independence the year before, 1956, but is often seen as part of the Middle Eastern and North African sphere, especially given the nation's preponderant Arab population in its Northern half.

# AFTERMATH & LEGACY

The difficulties of creating national unity in the newly independent state took on even more serious dimensions during the early 1960s. Because each of the three regions had its own government, parliament, prime minister, and so forth, confusion arose about who was responsible for national affairs. Relationships among the various government leaders were complicated. Many of the more optimistic expectations for independence were frustrated. The gap between the wealthy elite and the mass of the population grew wider in the first few years, and politicians seemed to be more interested in enriching themselves and their families than in developing the nation. Many among the political elite were also disappointed by the conservative line of Balewa in international affairs. These frustrations, coupled with regionalism and ethnic divisiveness, built toward a crisis.

In the over thirty years since independence, Nigeria has experienced a bewildering number of governments, political parties, and leading politicians. Although the lists of names and parties may seem hopelessly complex, the overall picture has remained fairly clear. The regional, ethnic, and religious lines of division, reinforced during the colonial period, have dominated political events over this period. A second clear generalization is that military coups and governments recur with ominous regularity. Each attempt at restoring civilian, democratic government has so far been unsuccessful. These two generalizations should stand out clearly in the following sections.

## Divisions in Newly Independent Nigeria

As noted at the end of the previous chapter, no political party won a majority in the 1959 elections, but the Northern Peoples' Congress (NPC) was dominant with 142 seats. The two largest parties formed a coalition, with the NPC holding ten cabinet posts and the eastern NCNC party seven. Azikiwe chose to align his party with the NPC rather than the Action Group of Chief Awolowo (the AG) because he believed that the NCNC was more likely to win elections in the west than in the Hausa-Fulani dominated north; if he had allied with the AG, the NCNC could not have competed against them for votes. Also, such an East-West alliance would further harden the North-South split, while there were still at least two million Igbo living and working in the Northern Region. In other words, Azikiwe feared that exacerbating divisiveness between north and south might endanger Igbos living in the northern region. When this government was established on October 1, 1960, Nigeria became the fourth most populous member of the British Commonwealth, after India, Pakistan, and the UK itself.

In 1962 the completion of a new census of the population triggered a crisis. The census was a hot political issue in Nigeria because it determined the representation of the various regions in the national government. The last census in the 1950s had indicated that the Northern Region had a slightly larger population than both the southern regions combined. The Southerners questioned this result, fearing domination by the conservative, Hausa-Fulani north. When it began to appear that the new census would continue to give the advantage to the Northern Region, controversy erupted resulting in the dissolution of the coalition between the NCNC and the NPC.

Meanwhile further trouble developed in the Western Region. Awolowo hoped that the Action Group could become a truly national party, contesting seats in all three regions of the country, while Awolowo's deputy believed that the AG should concentrate on holding onto power in the west and cooperate with the national coalition at the federal level. The rivalry between the two men is representative of divisions present in all the regions. (It would be a mistake, in other words, to view each of the regions as wholly monolithic, even within ethnic groups). The regional and more conservative agenda of Awolowo's rivals was backed by traditional Yoruba rulers and wealthy businessmen, as well as the more traditional religious hierarchy. Conservative support came largely from the central and northern Yoruba areas such as Ilorin, Oyo, and Ife. Awolowo, on the other hand, had strong support in the southern areas (sometimes referred to as the more "modernized" areas) of

Ijebu, Egba, Benin, and some other areas that became part of the Midwest Region in 1963. The NPC led by the Sardauna, Ahmadu Bello, favored the more traditional side in this contest and provided support for Awolowo's opponents.

Awolowo and his Action Group were seen as a threat by the national ruling coalition of the NPC and NCNC. This threat was partly answered by the decision taken in 1962 to create the new Midwestern Region, carved out of an area that had been supportive of Awolowo in the Western Region. In late September, the chief and about thirty other AG activists were charged with treason, growing out of demonstrations Awolowo had organized to protest actions of the central government favoring his political rivals. On November 2, 1962, Chief Awolowo was sentenced to ten years in prison as a result of these charges, leading to a further split in the AG party.

On October 1, 1963, three years after independence, a new constitution replaced the Queen of Great Britain as Head of State with a new Federal President, a post given to the grand old man, Nnamdi Azikiwe. New elections, set for 1964, were called for under the new constitution. They would be contested by the new party alliances that were forming as a result of the controversies over the census and over the split in the AG following the trial and sentencing of Awolowo.

Two new national political parties were formed. First there was the NNA (Nigerian National Alliance) under the presidency of Sir Ahmadu Bello (the Sardauna of Sokoto). The NNA was an alliance of the NPC of the north and the new party comprising opponents of Awolowo in the West. Second, the UGPA (United Grand Progressive Alliance), combined the eastern-based NCNC under the leadership of Michael Okpara, who was premier of the Eastern Region, and the AG of Chief Awolowo. In the end, the UGPA disputed the legitimacy of the election procedures and largely boycotted the elections. The new parliament was dominated by the NNA and its allies, with the UGPA in opposition. Note that these so-called new parties largely perpetuated the divisions of the former political parties.

Azikiwe had to ask Balewa to form the government again. Violence broke out throughout the Western Region the following year (1965) as elections were held there for the regional parliament. It appears that the Sardauna of Sokoto made an effort to support, allegedly through illegal means, the conservative opponents of Awolowo. When two different results were announced, it became clear that law and order had broken down in that part of the country.

## The First Coups and Civil War: The First Decade

Under these circumstances of disorder and confusion a group of army majors, mostly Igbo and led by the Igbo Major Chukwuma Nzeogwu, staged a military coup on the night of January 14–15, 1966, in which Tafewa Balewa, the Sardauna Ahmadu Bello, and the Prime Minister of the Western Region, along with many high-ranking army officers, were murdered. When the majors were unable to establish a government, the remaining high officers named themselves the government with General I.T.U. Aguiyi-Ironsi, also an Igbo, the leader. The new National Military Government suspended the constitution of 1963 and placed military governors over each of the regions.

In May General Ironsi abolished the regions as governmental units in an effort to replace the federal system with a unitary state. Nigeria became simply the Republic of Nigeria, instead of the Federal Republic of Nigeria. All political parties were outlawed and the formation of new parties prohibited for the time being.

When Ironsi's government failed to punish the mostly Igbo majors for the murders in the coup, and when he promulgated a centralized governmental system which was seen as favoring the better educated Southerners over Northerners, the Northern Region erupted. Attacks on Igbo occurred throughout the north; thousands were killed and thousands more began to stream back toward the Igbo land in the Eastern Region. In July, Ironsi himself was killed on a visit to Ibadan in a northern-led counter-coup. On August 1, 1966 Yakubu Gowon, a lieutenant-colonel from one of the small ethnic groups of the middle belt, became the new head of state. The military governor of the Eastern Region, Lieutenant-Colonel Odumegwu Ojukwu, refused to recognize Gowon as head of state or head of the military. During September and October of that year there were reports of as many as 30,000 Igbo people killed in the Northern Region, while perhaps two million people fled as refugees into the Eastern Region.

Gowon wished to maintain a strong central government, while the eastern region under Ojukwu favored a looser confederation. The various factions held a conference in Ghana in early January of 1967, the results of which were inconclusive. In May 1967 Gowon made an attempt to break up the regional groupings that had caused so much trouble by creating twelve new states which cut across the old boundaries and seemed to eliminate the power of the former regions. Ojukwu rejected this plan and immediately declared the Eastern Region to be the independent Republic of Biafra on May 30, 1967 (although the Eastern Region had been acting as an autonomous state since March). While most of the Igbo of the Eastern Region appeared to support secession, many of the coastal and rivers people of the south—the old People of the Salt Water—did not. As further complication, oil had been discovered in the coastal region and was becoming an important income producer for Nigeria.

By June 14 Biafra had been blockaded by the federal navy. War did not really break out until July of 1967, at which time initial attacks on Biafra were beaten back. In the early stages of the war, Biafran forces were even able to invade the Mid-Western Region, but the superior numbers of the federal forces began to tell on the encircled Biafrans. The civil war over Biafran secession lasted for three long, very bloody years. Near war's end the federal blockade of the Igbo heartland was portrayed as an effort to starve the rebels into submission when the Ojukwu government hired the international public relations firm of Markpress of Geneva to play up charges of imposed starvation and genocide. World public opinion became a major force in the struggle. Gowon's government, aware of the propaganda, tried to find a way to let in food and medical relief, but the effort was unsuccessful because the Biafrans preferred relief by airlift while the Nigerian government favored land corridors through contested areas.

As the Nigerian civil war became an international issue, various nations took sides. Great Britain supported and provided military assistance to the federal government forces, as did the Soviet Union. France and South Africa tended to give rhetorical comfort and in some cases tangible support (through smuggled arms) to the Biafran forces. The South African government policy may have been motivated by a desire to weaken the potentially strongest Black African nation, an opponent of South Africa's apartheid. It is not clear why France under DeGaulle supported Biafra, except perhaps as part of a policy intended to weaken the most important English-speaking state in West Africa. Richard Nixon, who became President of the United States in 1969, seemed to favor recognition of Biafra and a major American role in mediating an end to the conflict. On the other hand, Henry Kissinger, Nixon's influential Secretary of State, did not want the conflict to distract American attention from what he considered more important matters, such as settling the war in Vietnam. The State Department always appeared to favor the federal side in the war. As a result of these divisions, the U.S. took a basically neutral position. Among African states, only four recognized Biafra during the war: Tanzania and Zambia (anglophone, former British colonies), and Gabon and Ivory Coast (francophone states in West Africa).

Gradually, the federal army encircled the last remaining pockets of Biafran resistance in the heart of Igbo country. Gowon made a major effort to prevent any mistreatment of the Igbo people outside the Biafran controlled zones. Azikiwe indicated the success of this policy of Gowon when the NCNC leader flew into Lagos and proclaimed that he did not believe that the federal government would permit massacres of the Igbos following the war. In January of 1970, following thirty months of civil war, Ojukwu fled the country, leaving a second-in-command to announce that Biafra had ceased to exist. Former rebel officers and civil servants were allowed to resume their posts, and food relief was vigorously stepped up. The government quickly issued seeds and farm tools throughout the Eastern Region to begin rebuilding the agricultural base. Gowon and the victorious federal army showed themselves to be magnanimous and conciliatory, and fears of retaliation were allayed. The Nigerian Civil War is still remembered as one of the major tragedies of newly independent Africa, however.

The ordeals of Nigeria in its first decade of independence (the 1960s) are representative of the problems facing all new African nations, which can be summarized as follows:

1. *Economic infrastructure born to serve colonial rather than local interests.* Road and railway systems, for example, were built to facilitate the extraction of raw materials from the colony, rather than to link Nigeria to a wider West African market. These roads, therefore, all run north and south.

2. *Political weaknesses engendered by restrictions on natural political development under indirect rule.* Colonial rule sought not to develop political leaders who could take over the administration of the whole nation.

3. *Over-emphasis on ethnic and regional politics in the colonial, as well as the early independent phases of national life.* This emphasis derived from a divide-and-conquer policy. The difficulties in forging a national consciousness from such disparate groups are found throughout the continent.

The whole point of establishing colonies in the first place was to provide markets and cheap raw materials for the metropolitan power. In other words, colonization was for the benefit of Great Britain, France, Belgium, Portugal, and other imperial powers. As a result, the new nations, as former colonies, were unprepared to establish the institutional and economic bases for nationhood.

## The Second Decade: the Coups Continue

In Nigeria, as throughout Africa, the frustrations with the political process have led to a series of military coups and military governments. After his military victory in 1970, Gowon announced that there would be a return to civilian rule in 1975. Just before that date, however, Gowon himself was overthrown in another military coup. Coups have continued, followed by efforts to restore civilian elections, followed by more coups.

In the 1970s, Nigeria began to play a stronger role in Africa and in international affairs. In the second decade of independence, oil production began, and Nigeria became the seventh largest oil-producer in the world and is now a major supplier to the United States. Nigeria expanded its oil market during the days of the 1973 Arab-led embargo on oil shipments to the Western countries occasioned by the 1973 so-called "Yom Kippur" War between Israel and the Arab states.

Unfortunately, the first half of the 1970s was also marked by increased corruption and diversion of public funds for private use. The state governors under Gowon were particularly notorious for alleged misuse of power and public funds. The professional army commanders who had helped win the civil war and who had been instrumental in bringing Gowon to power lost respect for the federal president during this time. The leader of these commanders was Murtala Mohammed. A clash concerning national oil policy seemed to precipitate the coup that overthrew Gowon in 1975. Mohammed represented a group of young and professionally oriented administrators known as the "Kaduna Mafia." Although drawn from the conservative north with links to the aristocratic Hausa-Fulani, this group was also nationalist and reformist.

The new government of the SMC (Supreme Military Council) under Mohammed had to deal with the continuing divisive issues of a new 1973 population census, the issue of return to civilian rule, and the creation of new federal capital in the middle of the country at Abuja. Although Mohammed was the leader, the SMC represented a collegial type of rule, which meant that when Mohammed was assassinated in an abortive coup in 1976, the new supreme ruler, General Olesugun Obasanjo, could pick up and continue most of the same policies. The assassination of Mohammed, therefore, did not mean a change in regime or government policy. The government continued to move against corrupt officials from the former military regime: ten of the former twelve state governors were found guilty of massive corruption, and in "Operation Deadwoods" about 10,000 public employees were dismissed for abuse or corruption in office.

Under a military government the constitution is usually suspended if not abolished outright. Nigeria's first military government under Gowon took over legislative, executive, and even judicial functions for a time. In 1970, by a decree of the military government, the judiciary regained its independence and remained more or less independent under the Mohammed-Obasanjo regimes, as well. As usual in military government, laws were enacted by decree of the supreme commander instead of by the legislature, and each region was administered by an appointed military governor. Of course, the military could not govern alone: the civil service was required to handle the day-to-day affairs and operations. Hence, the military formed a sort of partnership with the civil servants as well as some important business leaders. A national-level executive council discussed some policy and included some civilian representation.

To increase its control, the Mohammed-Obasanjo government expanded the number of states from the twelve established under Gowon to nineteen (there were 30 by 1994). A larger number of states, it was hoped, would decrease the regional hegemony of the major ethnic groups which had bedeviled Nigerian politics so far. In addition, each state, being smaller and less self-sufficient, would be more dependent upon the central government. Through its control of oil revenues, which by 1975–76 had become 93% of Nigeria's total export income, the central government had accumulated a great deal of income which it could distribute as largess. The increase in the number of states also resulted in a great expansion of the bureaucracy with nineteen state administrations in place of the original three at the time of independence.

## The Second Republic: Return to Civilian Government

The military, when they take power in Africa, generally see their rule as temporary, a corrective to remedy the ills of an unpopular or corrupt civilian political regime. In a sense, the temporary nature of military governments allows for a form of permanence. Since it is conceivable that civilian regimes will always need correction, the military can always return to power. This pattern has repeated itself not only in Nigeria but in Ghana, Uganda, Mali, and many other African states in the thirty years since independence.

When Mohammed came to power, he immediately announced plans to return Nigeria to civilian rule. After Mohammed's death, Obasanjo held to these plans and the initial time table, which saw elections for a civilian government in 1979. The military government insisted on laying down the rules for political participation in the new republic. After all, the military did not want a civilian government that would be too different ideologically from its own regime. Some have argued that this "ideology" was virtually an absence of ideology because control of the government was mainly seen as a way to gain access to wealth for the favored military, civil service, and business elites. An important feature of the transfer of power was the control over the formation of new political parties for contesting the elections of 1979. A federal commission would determine which parties could participate legitimately in the process.

A constituent assembly started work on the constitution in December of 1976. This body was largely a collection of "wise men," including many former politicians, important businessmen, lawyers, university professors, and other members of the political and economic elite. For the most part, peasants, farmers, labor unions, students, and women were excluded from the constitution-making process. The new constitution, completed in 1978, increased the powers of the central government in comparison with the pre-1966 constitution, following the tendency of the military governments.

There was a system of checks and balances among the legislative, executive, and judiciary branches, as in the American constitution. In addition to the civil rights of individuals such as freedom of religion and speech, there were to be socioeconomic rights which were considered "communal" as distinct from individual. These communal rights included rights to education, economic development, and a just economic order. It was decided, however, that these economic rights were to be considered long-range goals and therefore not capable of being enforced by courts in law. That is, while a Nigerian may seek redress in the courts for a violation of individual rights, he or she cannot go to the courts because "communal" rights have been violated.

After some minor modifications by the military administration, the 1979 constitution became the basis for the elections of 1979 and the return to civilian rule. To an outsider, the election campaign of 1979 appears very complicated because of the number of different political parties involved, their constituencies, and shifting alliances and coalitions. The following details may seem daunting, but they do serve to convey an overall impression of Nigerian politics during this period.

Before proceeding, one needs to understand two rules laid down for the national election. The successful candidate for president needed to do more than simply get more votes than his rivals (all the candidates were male). To show a national constituency, the winning candidate had to receive at least one-fourth of the votes cast in at least two-thirds of the 19 states. Secondly, only political parties approved by the Federal Election Commission could field candidates. This second rule meant that only recognized, registered parties could participate, freezing out independent candidates or those from special interest groups such as labor unions.

The most powerful party was the National Party of Nigeria (NPN), which attempted to set up a national organization, although its fundamental power was in the north (similar to the old NPC). Getting an even earlier start was the UPN (United Party of Nigeria), formed hours after the ban on political parties was lifted. This party was headed by Chief Awolowo, whose writings and speeches provided its basic platform, and it remained identified with the Yoruba of the west. Attempts were made to appeal to minority ethnic groups in all regions by the formation of still more, smaller parties.

Finally, Azikiwe again entered the contest, leading to the establishment of a new party based largely on Igbo support. Again, the parties approximated the original three divisions of North, West, and East present at the time of Independence.

The NPN was most successful in attracting funding and powerful regional leaders, who saw advantage in being on the winning team. The national results of the 1979 elections bore out this success. Shehu Shagari, the nominee of the NPN, placed first or second in the balloting of eighteen of the nineteen states, received at least one-fourth of the votes in each state. While Awolowo was not far behind in total votes (his 4.9 million to Shagari's 5.7 million), a huge percentage of his votes—4.3 million of his total—came in four Yoruba dominated states. The local and state elections revealed the continuing power of ethnic and regional politics.

During the first Shagari administration, economic conditions worsened. The world oil glut led to a significant decline in export revenues, while growing corruption and inefficiency siphoned off state funds from development, education, and other services. Because the NPN was based on an ability to deliver "chop" (payoffs, bribes, and the like) to notables and party stalwarts, the decline in national income also weakened the party's political power. As one authority puts it, "Even while politicians continued to consume flagrantly, raise their personal emoluments and live in an unprecedentedly lavish style . . . , the population were subject to worker 'retrenchments,' higher taxes, declining services, and inflation."[1]

Under these conditions of economic distress and growing discontent, the 1983 elections went forward. The NPN, now in control of the government, could use its muscle to weaken opponents by excluding some factions or candidates and by buying off potential opponents. Candidates began shifting from party to party in an effort to find a slot in a winning combination; such shifting was easy because parties were for the most part not based on ideological differences or programs. Basically, the same parties and candidates from 1979 competed in the 1983 elections, but party lines and positions became so unclear that the results are difficult to analyze on a party-by-party basis. In the event, Shagari and the NPN seemed to win overwhelmingly (if not convincingly, given charges of rigging, vote fraud, and so on) over Awolowo and Azikiwe, who were both now in their 70s.

**MAJOR POLITICAL PARTIES FROM INDEPENDENCE TO 1992**

| Name | Regional/Ethnic Assoc. | Leader |
|---|---|---|
| National Council of Nigeria and the Cameroons (NCNC); later National Council of Nigerian Citizens | Eastern/Igbo | Nnamdi Azikiwe |
| Northern Peoples Congress (NPC) | Northern/Hausa-Fulani | The Sardauna of Sokoto, Sir Ahmadu Bello |
| Action Group (AG) | Western/Yoruba | Chief Obafemi Awolowo |
| Nigerian National Alliance (largely continuation of NPC) | Northern/Hausa-Fulani | The Sardauna of Sokoto |
| United Grand Progressive Alliance (UGPA) (combination of NCNC and AG) | Western/Yoruba & Eastern/Igbo | Chief Awolowo & Michael Okpara |
| National Party of Nigeria (NPN; similar to NPC) | Northern/Hausa-Fulani | Shehu Shagari |
| United Party of Nigeria (UPN) | Western/Yoruba | Chief Awolowo |

## Military Government Re-Established

The government newly elected in the Summer of 1983 lasted only to the end of the year. On December 31, 1983, the military under General Mohammed Buhari announced that they were again taking over. Buhari intended to reassert discipline in political life, rooting out incompetence, mismanagement, and corruption. In that light his regime was seen as a successor to the popular but short-lived Murtala Mohammed regime. Lazy or incompetent civil servants were fired (or, in at least some cases, caned) and corrupt politicians were investigated and charged. As before, then, the purpose of military intervention in politics was to clean up the mess but not to make fundamental changes in the economic system. It now appears that several coups were being planned in the final stages of the Shagari administration, and that Buhari's may have been the first launched in order to forestall more junior and more radical officers. In fact, there were rumors of a failed anti-Buhari coup by lower-ranking officers within the first hundred days of his takeover.

While on the surface the Buhari coup seemed intended to correct many of the economic problems of the Shagari government, in reality Buhari continued many of his predecessor's economic policies, even enacting the annual budget for 1984 as drawn up by Shagari. In addition Buhari acted to comply with repayment and economic austerity packages being imposed by international lenders and the International Monetary Fund (IMF). Still, Buhari found some of the stricter "conditionalities" of the World Bank unacceptable and turned down a $3 billion loan needed to cover Nigeria's balance of payments deficit for 1983–84. The result was austerity with no sign of improving economic development. The government became increasingly repressive, instituting the death penalty (by firing squad) for a wide range of offenses.

As repression grew under Buhari, many factions within the military became disillusioned. On August 27, 1985, the army chief-of-staff, Ibrahim Babangida, overthrew Buhari's government. Babangida revealed himself to be a more conciliatory and effective leader than Buhari. The new president, occasionally described as a "soldier's soldier," also appears to have had more credibility and support within the military itself.

After coming to power, Babangida began planning for a 1992 return to civilian rule. The process was similar to that followed by the Obasanjo regime in preparation for the 1979 establishment of the Second Republic. In addition to setting up a constituent assembly to draft the new 1992 constitution, he instituted a Center for Democratic Studies for the purpose of training new politicians in democratic principles and procedures. In order to avoid some of the earlier problems with elective politics in Nigeria, Babangida also banned "old breed" politicians, that is all politicians who participated in the First or Second Republic.

Control over the election process was even tighter than in 1979. At first, a federal election commission was to approve two (and only two) political parties for contesting the elections, but when none seemed to meet the criteria of the military government, Babangida decided to create two "grassroots" parties by decree. The two created parties were the National Republican Convention (NRC), which was to be slightly to the right of center, and the Social Democratic Party (the SDP), just slightly to the left of center. The NRC generally drew support from the North, while the SDP tended to draw most of its support from the South.

After several false starts, two presidential candidates were selected, both of whom had close business and personal ties with President Babangida. In June 1993, elections for a national president were finally held and seemed to go smoothly, according to international and press observers. Although preliminary reports indicated that the Social Democratic candidate, Moshood Abiola, a wealthy media owner and a Muslim Yoruba, had won handily, Babangida stepped in and nullified the elections and their results. The general ultimately handed power over to a handpicked civilian president, Ernest Shonekan, in August of 1993. In the Fall of 1993, however, General Sani Abacha, long associated with various military governments, staged yet another coup, returning Nigeria to the same situation of military government endured so many times before.

General Abacha's rule was even more oppressive than earlier military governments. His government created an international uproar when they executed by hanging the well-known poet Ken Saro-Wiwa and eight of his colleagues active in a movement to protest human rights and environmental violations against their ethnic group, the Ogoni. Although a small group, the Ogoni live in the region of the Niger Delta dominated by the oil industry, represented by international firms such as the Royal Dutch/Shell Group and the Chevron Corporation. The Nobel-laureate Wole Soyinka was forced into exile for fear of imprisonment or even execution by the same Abacha regime. The apparent winner of the 1993 presidential election, Moshood Abiola, continued to languish in jail despite reported poor health and the murder of his senior wife. The widely-respected former military president, Olesugun Obasanjo, along with other respected leaders, remained in prison as well. In March 1998, Pope John Paul II visited Nigeria and called upon Abacha to release the leading political prisoners. International protests continued to grow even though Abacha promised a return to civilian government, albeit with many qualifications and restrictions.

In the summer of 1998 the sudden, unexpected death of Abacha, followed a month later by the death of Moshood Abiola, while still in custody, seemed to brighten the prospects for the political future of Nigeria. By October of 1998, conditions had so improved under the new military ruler, Abdulsalam Abubakar, with the release of most of the major dissidents from prison, that Wole Soyinka returned to Nigeria to essentially a hero's welcome. As 1998 draws to a close, there is hope for an early end to the latest military government and a return to democratic, civilian rule.

The table below indicates the dominance of the military and the Hausa-Fulani from the North in national politics since independence up to 1994.

**RULERS OF INDEPENDENT NIGERIA**

| Name | Years | Mil./Civ. |
|---|---|---|
| Sir Abubakar Tafewa Balewa (Hausa-Fulani) | 1960–66 | Civilian |
| I.T.U Aguiyi-Ironsi (Igbo) | 1966 | Military |
| Yakabu Gowon (Middle Belt) | 1966–75 | Military |
| Murtala Mohammed (Hausa-Fulani) | 1975–76 | Military |
| Olesugun Obasanjo (Yoruba) | 1976–79 | Military |
| Alhaji Shehu Shagari (Hausa-Fulani) | 1979–83 | Civilian |
| Muhammed Buhari (Hausa-Fulani) | 1983–85 | Military |
| Ibrahim Babangida (Hausa-Fulani) | 1985–93 | Military |
| Ernest Shonekan (Yoruba) | 1993 | Civilian (Military appointed) |
| Sani Abacha (Hausa-Fulani) | 1993-98 | Military |
| Abdusalam Abubakar (Hausa-Fulani) | 1998– | Military |

## Prospects for the 1990s and Beyond

Nigeria's prospects for the future depend largely on the process for returning government to civilian control. The Babangida regime repeated many of the mistakes made by the Obasanjo government in setting up the late Second Republic. The military still appears to distrust direct public participation in the political process.

Restrictions on the formation of political parties and on participation by individuals (former politicians and office-holders were banned) mean that any sort of radical or ideologically based political party or candidate was nearly frozen out.

The economy continues to be dependent upon transnational corporations; about 70% of Nigerian foreign exchange earnings are sent out of the country by such companies. As in the colonial period, the economy is largely extractive, based now upon the extraction and export of oil. The country is also subject to potential economic hardships resulting from a structural adjustment program intended to fulfill conditions for World Bank loans. Nigeria's situation in this regard is representative of many countries in Africa and parts of Latin America and Asia today.

Nigeria will continue to suffer divisiveness along regional, ethnic, and religious lines. Often these lines of cleavage reinforce each other, as when the Islamic north is set against the non-Islamic south. Unfortunately, religious violence recently has arisen in the northern part of the country. Riots broke out in Zaria and other northern cities over claims that Christians were slaughtering pigs in slaughter houses also used by Muslims. In an effort to reduce cleavages along regional and ethnic lines, more and more states have been created, as shown on the map below. The Federal Capital Territory in the middle is the location of the new capital city of Abuja within a separate territory outside state boundaries, on the model of the District of Columbia in the United States.

[See Map J. Contemporary Nigerian States.]

In assessing the nature and significance of the ethnic divisions, we must remember that there are many ethnic groups in addition to the major three of Hausa-Fulani, Yoruba, and Igbo. Moreover, these three large groups are fairly recent constructs, identities growing primarily out of the colonial period, as we have seen throughout this text. Thus, none of the three major groups is ethnically homogeneous, and other differences—in religion, dress, occupation—persist both within and between groups.

The model for political culture in a new state such as Nigeria was a colonial government. That model was largely authoritarian, concerned more with control than with democracy. The new elites of African states, and particularly Nigerian elites, have taken over this authoritarian model and its overarching concern for control. The colonial model also emphasized the extractive economy and the use of the state apparatus for generating income (for the ruling European nation during the colonial period; for the politicians under the independent state). In a model of this kind political energy tends to focus on gaining access to wealth and privilege rather than on political programs, diverse economic development, or genuine ideological differences.

## Conclusions

Still, there is hope that Nigeria can become a strong and powerful state on the basis of new economic power. In economic resources and educational base, Nigeria is certainly better off than many other African states. The growing power of Nigeria is seen, for example, in the leading role the Nigerian military has taken in the West African multilateral effort to stabilize the chaotic situation in Liberia.[2]

The cultural heritage of the country is an additional source of strength. Some of the most outstanding universities in Africa are in Nigeria—Universities of Ibadan, Ife, and Nsukka, and Muhammed Bello University. Nigeria has one of the most outstanding artistic traditions of any state in Africa. Two of Nigeria's authors have become international literary figures: Chinua Achebe, recognized as the foremost African novelist for his masterpiece on the crisis of traditional society in the colonial era, *Things Fall Apart*, and Wole Soyinka, winner of the Nobel Prize for literature for his plays, poetry, essays, and biographical writings.

Many of the challenges facing Nigeria and Africa are summarized by a passage near the end of Achebe's novel about modern Africa, *A Man of the People*. A corrupt politician has been brought down as a result of his excesses. The Igbo said of him that he had "taken enough for the owner to see." The protagonist meditates on these words, the same that he had heard when villagers punished a petty thief in earlier days. "The owner was the village, and the village had a mind; it could say no to sacrilege," he thinks. "But in the affairs of the nation there was no owner, the laws of the village became powerless."[3] As Achebe's narrator implies, new political traditions must be forged to create a national sense of ownership. As we have seen, Africans have been adaptable throughout history—traditions have been changed; change has resulted in new traditions. Nigeria could be the leader among African states in carrying on this process.

## Notes

1 William D. Graf, *The Nigerian State: Political Economy, State Class and Political System in the Post-Colonial Era*, London: Heinemann Educational Books, 1988, p. 95.

2 *African Confidential*, 24 January 1992: 70% of troops and 80% of funding are from Nigeria, and the commander is now from Nigeria, replacing a Ghanaian general after the murder of Sammy Doe.

3 Achebe, Chinua, *A Man of the People* (Garden City, NJ: Anchor Books, 1967), pp. 140–14 1.

# NIGERIA CHRONOLOGY

| | |
|---|---|
| 300 B.C.E.–250 C.E. | Nok Culture |
| ca. 700–1076 | Empire of Ghana |
| ca. 900–1895 | Kanem-Borno Empire |
| 1080 | Ruler of Kanem-Borno converted to Islam |
| 1000–1200s | Early Hausa states; settlements at Ife, Oyo |
| ca. 1300–1897 | Empire of Benin |
| ca. 1230–1390 | Empire of Mali |
| 1324–25 | Hajj of Mansa Musa to Arabia |
| 1350s | Ibn Battuta's visit to Mali |
| 1415 | Beginning of Portuguese discoveries in West Africa |
| 1532 | Inauguration of trans-Atlantic slave trade |
| 1600s | Dutch and English displace Portuguese in West Africa |
| 1670s | Establishment of powerful Akan empire of Ashanti |
| ca. 1700 | Establishment of Empire of Dahomey |
| 1725 | Beginning of Fulani Islamic *jihads* in Sudan |
| 1765 | Beginning of Antislavery Movement in England |
| ca. 1770–89 | Reign of Alafin Abiodun of Oyo |
| 1772 | Mansfield Decision outlaws slavery in England |

| | |
|---|---|
| 1775–83 | War of American Independence |
| 1800 | Sierra Leone founded |
| 1804 | Start of the *Jihad* of Uthman dan Fodio |
| 1807 | Great Britain outlaws slave trade for subjects |
| 1808 | USA outlaws slave trade |
| 1817 | Muhammed Bello succeeds to Caliphate of Sokoto |
| 1820s | Yoruba Wars begin |
| 1822 | Liberia founded |
| 1827 | Establishment of Fourah Bay College in Freetown, Sierra Leone |
| 1861 | British establish Lagos as a Crown Colony |
| 1884–85 | The Congress of Berlin |
| 1890–1906 | British conquest of Nigeria |
| 1905–1920 | Establishment of Indirect Rule in Nigeria |
| 1914 | Amalgamation of Northern and Southern Nigeria |
| 1914–1918 | World War I |
| 1919, 1921, 1923 | First, Second and Third Pan-African Congresses |
| 1920s | Rise of Herbert Macaulay and the Nigerian National Democratic Party (NNDP) |
| 1923 | NNDP of Herbert Macaulay wins first election |
| 1938 | Azikiwe head of Nigerian Youth Movement |
| 1939–1945 | World War II |
| 1941 | Azikiwe organizes National Council of Nigeria and the Cameroons (NCNC) |

| | |
|---|---|
| 1946 | Abubakar Tafewa Balewa returns to Nigeria, heads the Northern Peoples' Congress (NPC) |
| 1949 | Obafemi Awolowo organizes the Action Group (AG) |
| 1954 | New constitution established leading to independence |
| 1959 | First national elections for independent government |
| Oct. 1, 1960 | Independence |
| 1964 | Elections on basis of new census; NPC gains majority; Balewa continues as Prime Minister |
| Jan. 1966 | First military coup, bringing Ironsi to power; anti-Igbo violence breaks out |
| July 1966 | Second military coup; Gowon in power |
| 1967–1970 | War of Biafran secession; Federal Government defeats Biafra |
| 1975 | Overthrow of Yakubu Gowon by Gen. Murtala Mohammed |
| 1976 | Mohammed assassinated; replaced by Gen. Obasanjo |
| 1979 | Civilian elections; President Shehu Shagari |
| 1983 | Shagari overthrown by Gen. Muhammed Buhari |
| 1985–1991 | Ibrahim Babangida overthrows Buhari |
| 1993 | Attempted Presidential election nullified by Babangida |
| | Moshood Abiola apparent winner |
| 1993 | Babangida appoints Ernest Shonekan President |

| | |
|---|---|
| 1993–1998 | Military coup of General Sani Abacha; military government |
| 1995 | Execution of internationally-known poet, Ken Saro-Wiwa and eight other leaders of Movement for Survival of the Ogoni people |
| June 8, 1998 | Death of Sani Abacha of unexpected heart attack; General Abubakar new president. |
| July 7, 1998 | Death of Moshood Abiola, apparent winner of election of 1993, while in custody of military government |

# MAPS

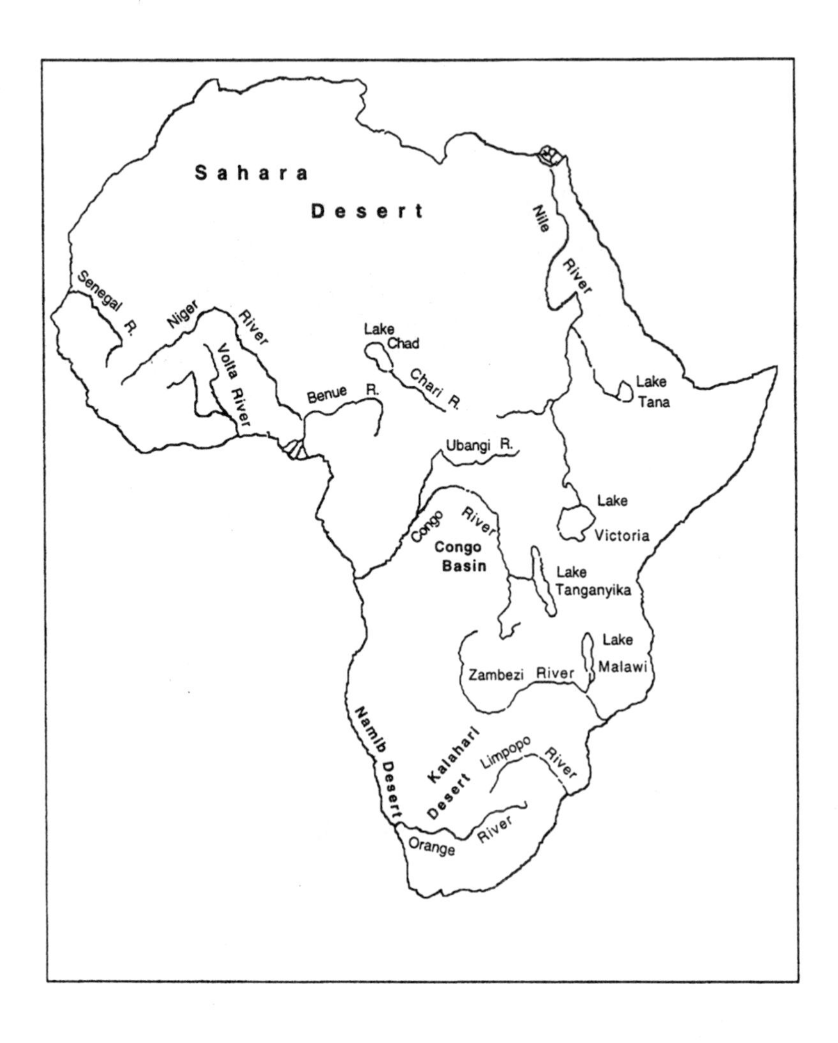


**Map A.
The African Continent**

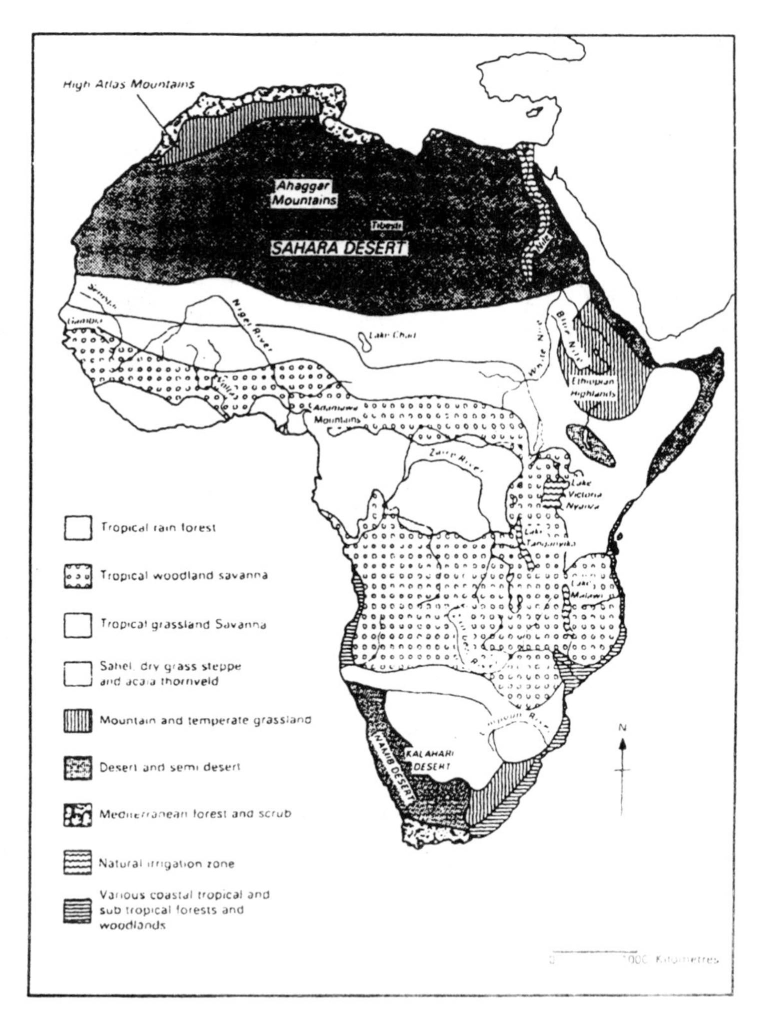


Source: *History of Africa* by Kevin Shillington. Copyright © 1989 by St. Martin's Press.

**Map B.**
**The Vegetation of Modern Africa**

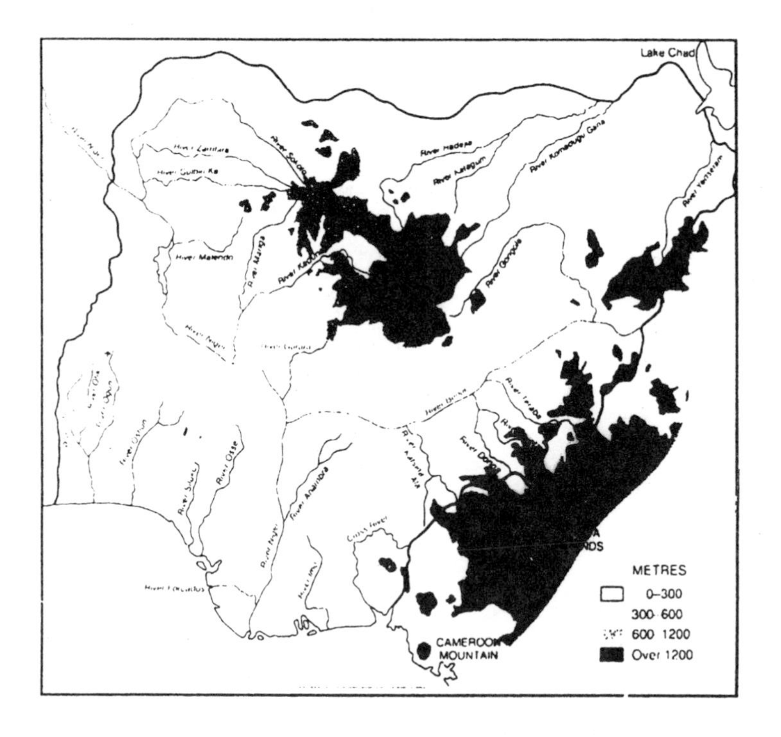


Source: *Nigeria: An Introduction to Its History* by Michael Crowder and Guda Abdullahi. Copyright © 1979 by Longman Group UK.

## Map C.
## Relief and Drainage in Nigeria

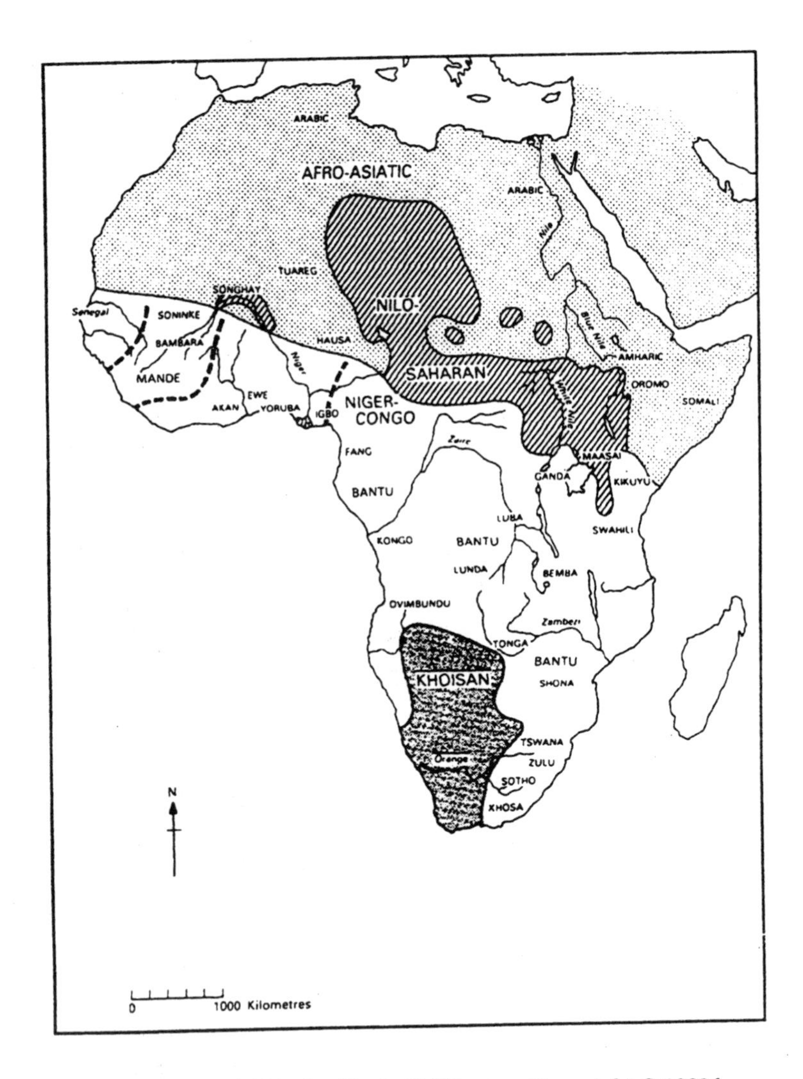


Source: *History of Africa* by Kevin Shillington. Copyright © 1989 by St. Martin's Press.

**Map D.**
**The Languages of Africa**

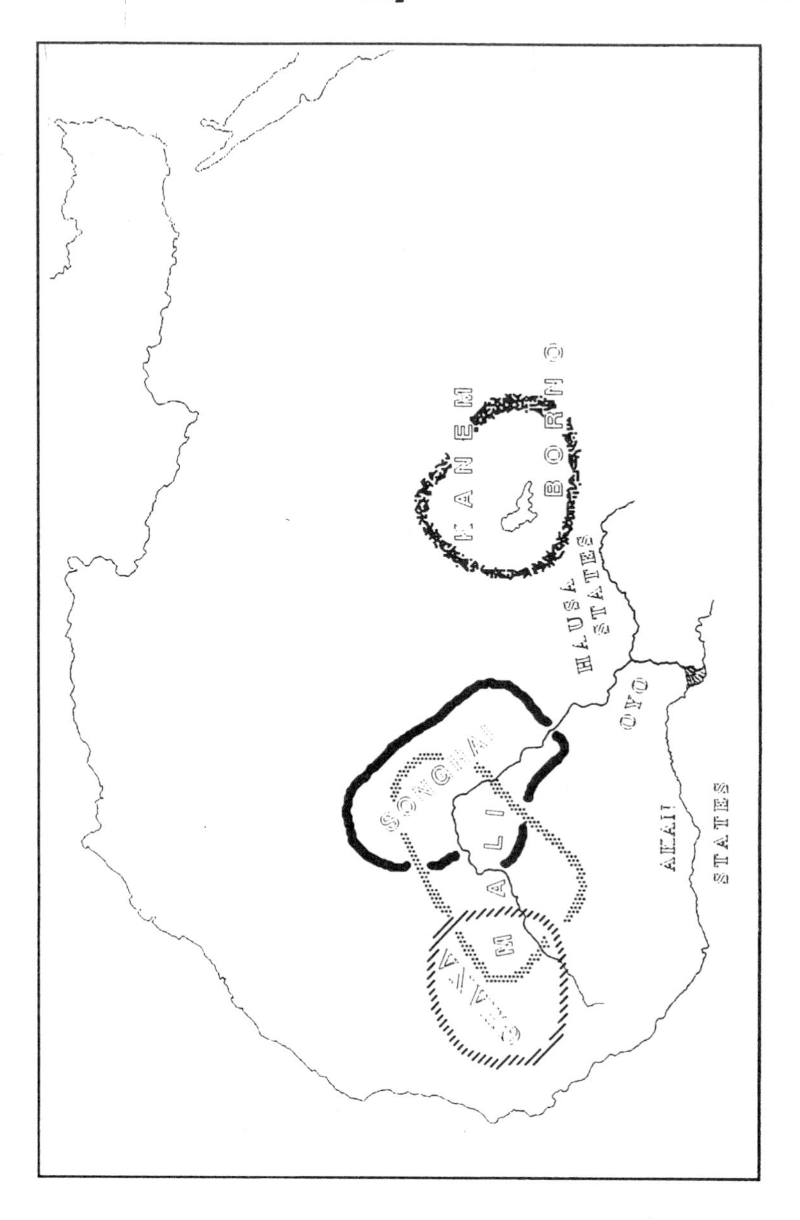


**Map E.**
**Contemporary Nigerian States**

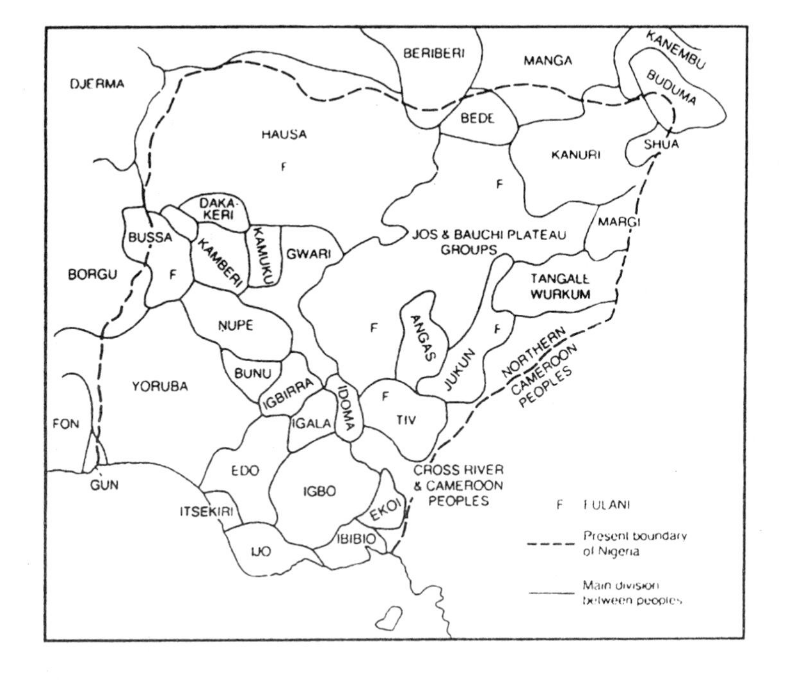


Source: *Nigeria: An Introduction to Its History* by Michael Crowder and Guda Abdullahi. Copyright © 1979 by Longman Group UK.

**Map F.**
**Major Ethnic Groups of Nigeria**

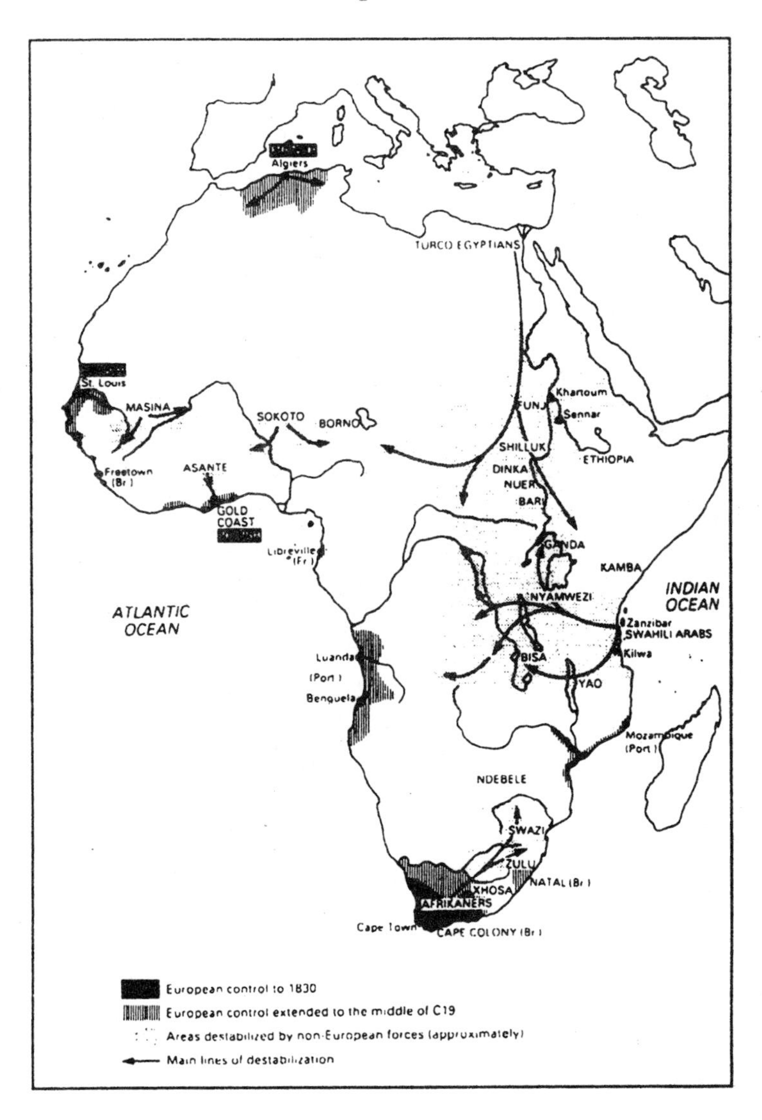


Source: *The African Experience* by Roland Oliver. Copyright © 1991 by HarperCollins.

**Map G.**

**The Opening Up and Destabilization of Africa, Mid-19th Century**

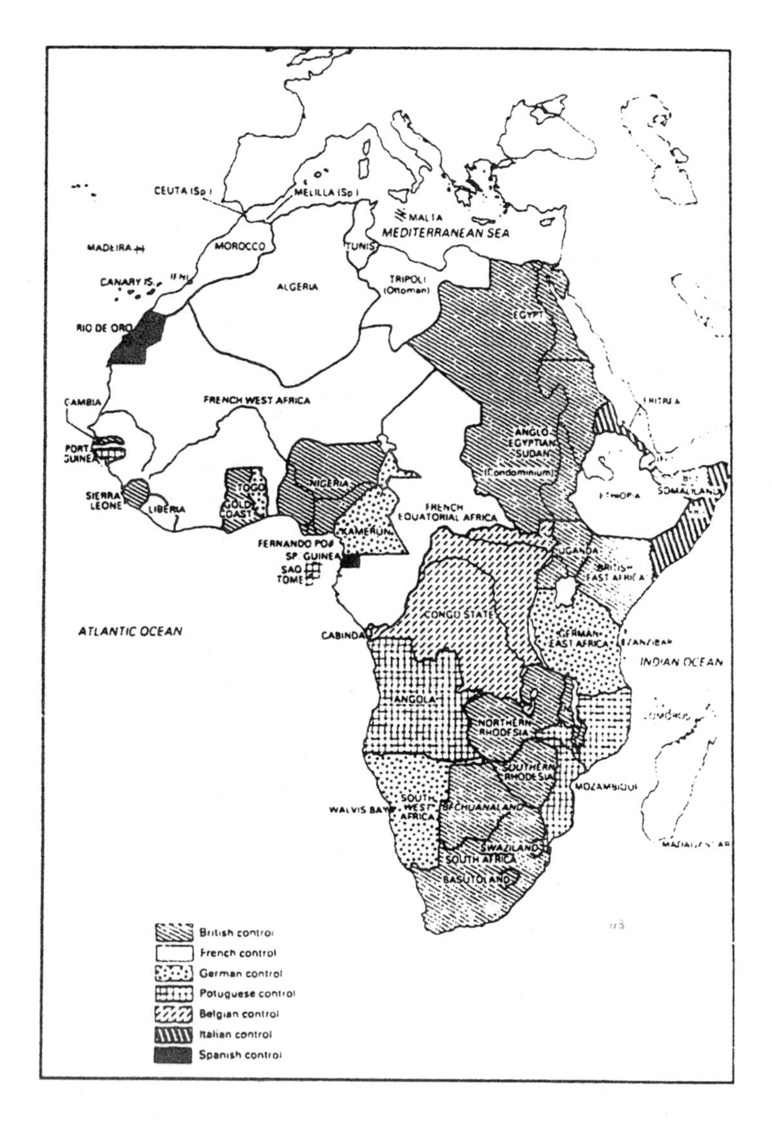


Source: *The African Experience* by Roland Oliver. Copyright © 1991 by HarperCollins.

**Map H.**

**The Map Completed, c. 1902**

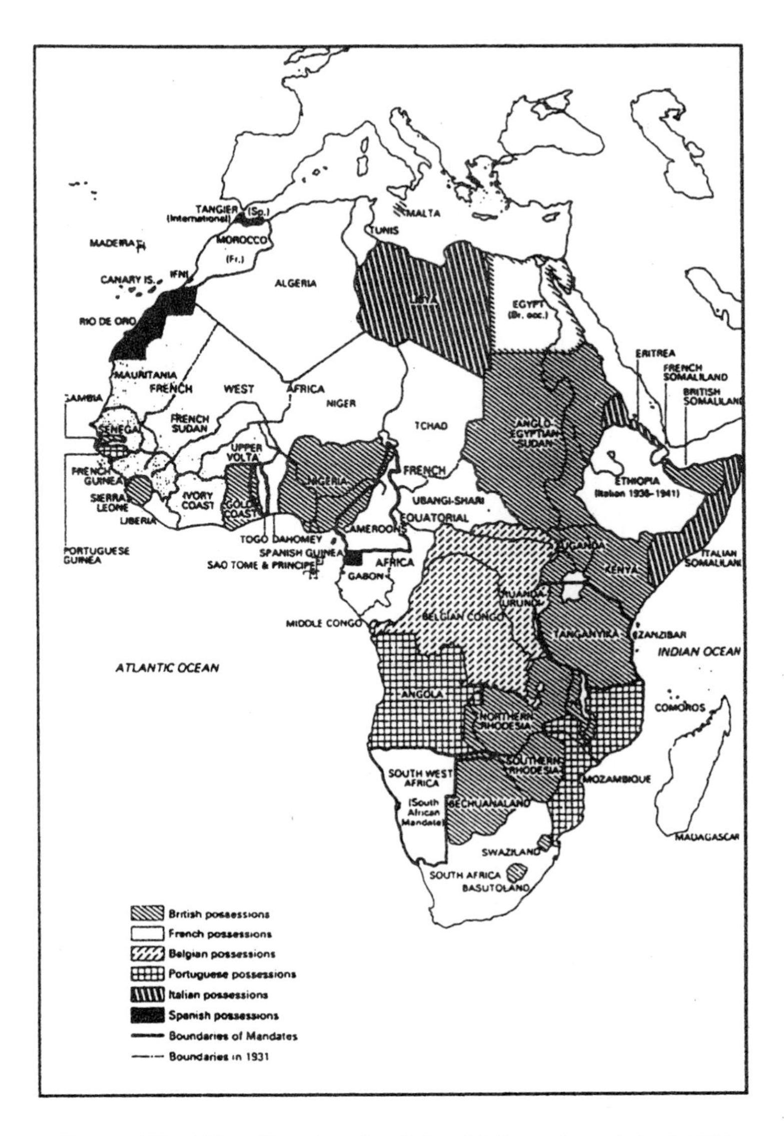


Source: *The African Experience* by Roland Oliver. Copyright © 1991 by HarperCollins.

## Map I.

## Colonial Africa between the Two World Wars